Brain Food

Games That
Make Kids Think

Paul Fleisher

illustrated by Patricia Keeler

Zephyr
Press ©

REACHING THEIR HIGHEST POTENTIAL

To Daniel and Martin,
my brothers
and first game-
playing companions.

Brain Food
Games That Make Kids Think

Grades: All ages

©1997 by Zephyr Press
Printed in the United States of America

ISBN 1-56976-072-1

Editor: Stacey Shropshire
Cover design: Daniel Miedaner
Illustrations: Patricia Keeler
Design and production: Daniel Miedaner

Zephyr Press
P. O. Box 66006
Tucson, AZ 85728-6006

Library of Congress Cataloging-in-Publication Data

Fleisher, Paul, 1951-
    Brain food : games that make kids think / Paul Fleisher.
        p.   cm.
    Includes bibliographical references (p.) and indexes.
    Summary: A compilation of thinking games requiring intelligence
skills, in such categories as "Spatial Orientation and Strategy
Games," "Alignment Games," "Capture Games," "Maze Games,"
"Mathematical Games," and "Word Games."
    ISBN 1-56976-072-1
    1. Educational games—Juvenile literature. [1. Games.]
I. Title.
GV1480.F54 1997
793.7—dc21   97-11695

Contents _____

Mathematical Operations

Factors and Multiples

Deductive Logic Games

Word Games

Spelling Games

Anagrams

Long Words

Other Vocabulary Builders

Puns and Other Word Play

Dramatic Word Games

Rhymes and Homonyms

Miscellaneous Word Games

Memory Games

Visual Arts Games

Bibliography

Alphabetical Index

Acknowledgments _____

Most of the games in this volume I've learned from others. Many are traditional games described in various other collections. Some I learned from my parents or teachers. Others I learned from teaching colleagues and educational journals or books I've read over the years.

I wish I could give specific credit for the original sources of each of these games. Unfortunately, I've not kept track of where I found each one. Nevertheless, I owe a great debt to many other writers who also love games and love to teach with them. I invite any reader who may know the original source of any of the unattributed games in this volume to contact me through Zephyr Press so I can give the creator of the game credit in future editions.

I would especially like to acknowledge the authors listed in the bibliography and to recommend their works. These writers have taught me new games and reminded me of others that I once knew and had since forgotten.

I would like to thank the students in my classes at Binford Middle School who helped me by testing games and suggesting refinements in the directions. Their contributions have been invaluable. I'd also like to thank Joe Parfitt for teaching me the game Huvnuts and Jolenn Williams for teaching me SOS.

I'd like to express special appreciation to my brother Martin, creator of 99 Syllables, and to Kate Miller, Genevieve Plentl, and Octavia Seigel-Hawley who created the game Face 2 Face. Both games appear for the first time in this volume.

And finally, I want to thank my wife, Debra Sims Fleisher, for her patience as I've worked on this project, and more importantly, for her love and support in all I do.

Introduction _____

Games give us a few moments of diversion from the weightier matters of life. They generate the excitement of competition and risk. Games provide a setting for pleasant interaction with friends. And some games are brain food. By their very nature, those games require us to think.

Of course, we don't develop our minds in the same way we develop our biceps. No simple, repetitive exercise will turn a child into a logical thinker. But game playing can teach children and adults to think more logically, analytically, and creatively. Anyone who has mastered a challenging new game knows how much mental "exercise" such an endeavor provides, and how satisfying that mastery can be.

The games you'll find in *Brain Food* call for a variety of higher level thinking processes and put a number of our multiple intelligences to use. Each game in this book requires players to analyze game situations, evaluate the effectiveness of actions and strategies, and create new strategies based on those evaluations.

Some—such as Coyote and Chickens or Alphamazement—require strategic thinking. Players must analyze the current game situation, then look ahead, evaluating the advantages and disadvantages of possible moves. Others—such as Nim or Taxman—call for the discovery of a guiding principle or method that will lead to success. Still others—such as Bagels or Twenty Questions—require pure deductive logic. Some games—Derrah or Crucible, for example—challenge a player's ability to manipulate spatial patterns. Ghost, Wordbuilder, and many others encourage vocabulary development. Dictionary and Arty Dots call for creative thinking and imagination.

When children play these games, they will find themselves using problem-solving and decision-making skills—the skills teachers and parents want them to develop so they can function effectively in the "real world." And what's even better, kids have fun while they're learning these skills.

One of the great benefits of playing games is that it helps children develop social skills. Even the most competitive games require cooperation. Players must agree to follow the rules, take turns, and accept the results of the game's outcome.

Game players develop a tolerance for the ebb and flow of fortune. Players learn to accept those players who are less skilled and to respect those whose skills are stronger. Stronger players serve as models for weaker ones. Games also help children develop a sense of fairness. Players learn that individual desires often have to give way to higher principles if the game is to succeed.

Playing the games in this book may not make you smarter. But they will put your brain power to good use. And I hope they'll serve as brain food, nourishing your thinking skills while you play. Bon appétit!

A Few General Notes _____

Choosing Who Will Play First

Most games require players to decide who will play first. Probably the easiest way to do this is for the players to agree on someone to be first player. One of the players may volunteer to go first, or suggest someone else for that honor. Of course, that doesn't always work. Fortunately, there are many other options for choosing; following are just a few:

> Flip a coin. Pick a hidden object in one or the other hand. Play rock/paper/scissors. Roll dice—high or low number plays first. Pick a card—low or high card plays first. Pick scrabble tiles—closest to A plays first. Youngest player plays first.

Whatever method you use should be quick, noncontroversial, and random, when appropriate. In subsequent rounds of the game, it is often a good idea to have the losing player go first and the winning player go last.

Tokens

Many of these games call for the use of game tokens. Any number of inexpensive and readily available objects such as beans, seeds, pebbles, coins, checkers, small erasers, shells, nuts, washers, or bottle caps will serve the purpose.

Word Games

A few standard rules apply to most word games:

- Use the best, most comprehensive dictionary you can find as judge. Use it to decide whether a certain word is a real word or is spelled correctly.

- Don't allow proper nouns or the adjective form of proper nouns. For example, neither *France* nor *French* may be used in a game of Ghost or Matrix.

- Don't allow words and phrases from languages other than the language in which you are playing the game unless the words have become part of that language. *Bonjour* and *gracias* would not be permitted in a game in which you are using English only. However, words such as *rendezvous* and *fiesta* would be. As always, let the dictionary be your guide.

- Don't allow abbreviations, contractions, or acronyms. Words must be spelled out completely. *Doesn't, he's, Tues., NY,* or *P. S.* should not be accepted. Neither should NASA, MOMA, or POTUS.

Pronoun Gender

In writing this book, I've been faced with the familiar problem of choosing which pronouns to use. Unfortunately, English doesn't have third person singular pronouns that refer to both sexes. I use the plural whenever possible and alternate between masculine and feminine pronouns in other places.

Let the Games Begin

Dots

Number of Players	2 to 4
Object	To create the most squares by drawing lines between adjacent dots on the playing board
Materials	copies of game board (page 6) pencils or pens
Playing the Game	1. Players decide who will play first. After the first game, the loser of the previous game goes first. Each player chooses a symbol—such as initials—to write inside completed squares. 2. Players take turns connecting two adjacent dots with either vertical or horizontal lines. 3. When a player draws the line that completes a square, she writes her symbol inside. 4. Completing a square gives a player another turn. A player continues with more turns as long as she completes squares. 5. The game is over when all squares on the game board have been enclosed. Players count the number of squares containing their symbols. The player who has the most squares is the winner.
Variation	This game may be played with various sizes of arrays of dots.

The Snake

Number of Players	2
Object	To be the last player to add a line to the snake without connecting to another part of the snake
Materials	copies of game board (page 6) pencils or pens
Playing the Game	1. Players decide who will play first. After the first game, the loser of the previous game plays first. 2. The first player starts the snake by connecting two adjacent dots on the game board. Only vertical or horizontal lines may be used. 3. The second player connects an adjacent dot to either end of the snake with a vertical or a horizontal line. 4. Players continue taking turns, adding to either end of the snake, one line at a time. 5. The last player to add a line to the snake without connecting to any other part of the snake is the winner.
Variation	This game may be played with various sizes of arrays of dots. Players may choose to play on a smaller array of dots to shorten the game.

Bonus Dots

Number of Players	2 to 4
Object	To score the most points by enclosing squares on the game board (players score extra points by enclosing squares with bonus points)
Materials	copies of game board (page 6) pencils or pens
Playing the Game	1. Players decide who will play first. After the first game, the loser of the previous game plays first. Each player chooses a symbol to write inside completed squares. 2. Before play begins, players take turns writing the numerals 1 to 20, in order, in potential squares on the game board. 3. Play proceeds like Dots. Players take turns connecting adjacent dots with vertical or horizontal lines. 4. When players enclose a square, they write their symbols inside. 5. Completing a square gives a player another turn. A player continues for as long as he completes squares. 6. The game is over when all squares on the game board have been enclosed. Players count the number of squares that contain their symbols, then add all bonus points they have enclosed to their point totals. The player with the highest score is the winner.
Variation	Before play begins, each player marks five squares with a unique symbol. Players earn 10 additional bonus points for each of their own symbols they enclose in a square. They lose 5 points for each of their opponents' symbols they enclose.

Superdots

Number of Players	2 to 4
Object	To score the most points by enclosing shapes on the game board
Materials	copies of game board (page 6) pencils or pens

Playing the Game

1. Players decide who will play first. After the first game, the loser of the previous game plays first. Each player creates a symbol to write inside complete shapes to claim them.

2. Players take turns connecting adjacent dots with vertical, horizontal, or diagonal lines.

3. When players enclose one of the scoring shapes (see figure 1), they write their symbols inside. The shapes are worth the points shown in figure 1. Once a shape has been claimed, it may not be divided into smaller shapes.

4. Only the scoring shapes may be claimed. Any other enclosed space may be subdivided until its parts are claimed.

5. Claiming a shape gives a player another turn. A player continues for as long as she continues to complete scoring shapes. Completing a small triangle does not score any points, but it does entitle the player to another turn.

6. The game is over when no more scoring shapes can be completed. Players tally the scores of the shapes that contain their symbols. The player with the highest score is the winner.

Figure 1. Scoring shapes for superdots

Game Board: Dots, The Snake, Bonus Dots, and Superdots

Tridots

Number of Players	2 to 3
Object	To enclose the largest number of triangles by drawing lines between adjacent dots on the game board
Materials	copies of game board (page 9) pencils or pens
Playing the Game	1. Players decide who will play first. After the first game, the loser of the previous game plays first. Each player creates a symbol to write inside completed triangles to claim them.
	2. Players take turns connecting adjacent dots with straight lines. A player may connect any two adjacent dots on the game board.
	3. Whenever players enclose a triangle, they write their symbols inside to claim them.
	4. Completing a triangle entitles a player to another turn. A player continues with more turns for as long as he continues to complete triangles.
	5. The game is over when all triangles on the game board have been enclosed and claimed. Players count the number of triangles that contain their symbols. The player who has claimed the most triangles is the winner.
Variation	This game may be played with arrays of dots of any size.

Hyperdots

Number of Players	2 to 4
Object	To score the most points by enclosing shapes on the game board
Materials	copies of game board (page 9)
	pencils or pens
Playing the Game	

1. Players decide who will play first. After the first game, the loser of the previous game plays first. Each player creates a symbol to write inside shapes to claim them.

2. Players take turns connecting adjacent dots with straight lines. A player may connect any two adjacent dots on the game board.

3. When players enclose one of the scoring shapes (below), they write their symbols inside to claim them. Once a shape has been claimed, it may not be subdivided into smaller shapes.

4. Only the scoring shapes may be claimed. Any other enclosed space may be subdivided until its parts are claimed.

5. Completing a scoring shape gives a player another turn. A player continues with more turns for as long as she continues to complete shapes. Completing a small triangle does not score any points. However, it does entitle the player to another turn.

6. The game is over when no more shapes can be claimed. Each player tallies the scores of all the shapes that contain her symbol. The player with the highest score is the winner.

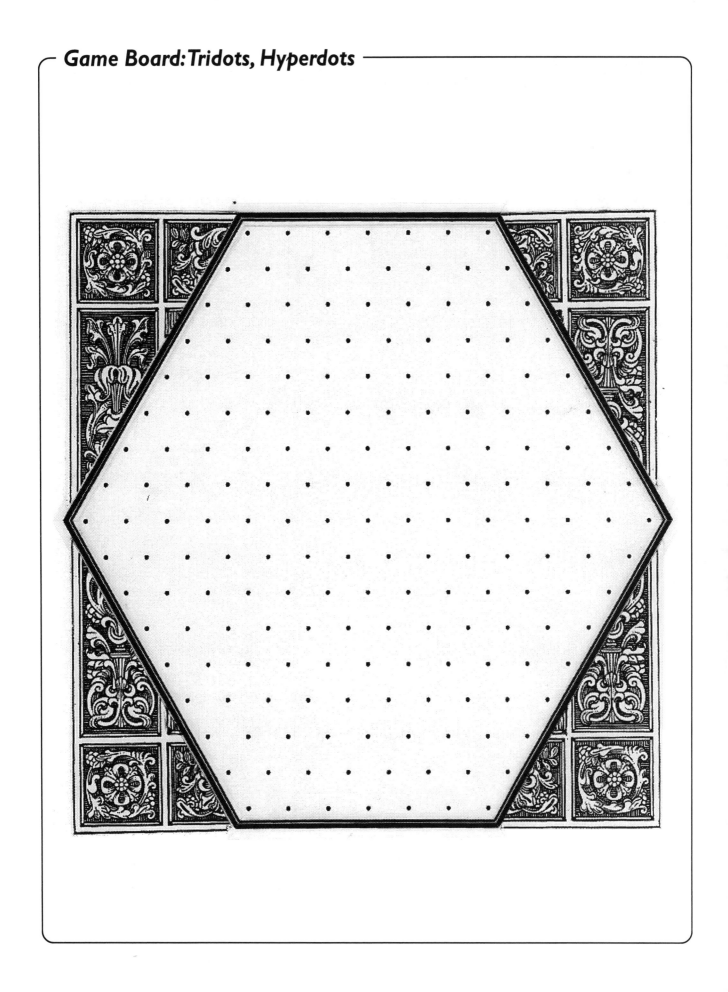

SOS

Number of Players	2
Object	To make the most SOS chains
Materials	copies of game board (page 11) or paper pencils
Playing the Game	1. Players decide what size game grid to use—4 by 4, 5 by 5, 6 by 6, or larger. Players also decide who will play first. After the first game, the loser of the previous game plays first.
	2. The first player writes either the letter S or the letter O in any square on the game board.
	3. The second player writes either a letter S or a letter O in any other square of the grid.
	4. Play continues in this manner. At each turn, a player may write either an S or an O. Each player attempts to complete the letter sequence SOS horizontally, vertically, or diagonally on the board while preventing the opponent from doing so. Players score one point for each SOS sequence they make.
	5. When a player forms the sequence SOS on the board, he draws a line through it and tallies a point for himself on the paper. Each time a player completes an SOS, he gets another turn.
	6. Letters on the game board may be used to make more than one SOS sequence. For example, an O that has been used as part of a horizontal SOS may later become part of vertical or diagonal SOS sequences, scoring additional points for the player who completes them.
	7. Play continues until all squares on the game board have been filled. The player who has tallied the most points is the winner.
Variation	This game is traditionally played with only two players. However, using a larger game grid, there's no reason why the game can't be played with 3 or 4 players.

Game Board: SOS

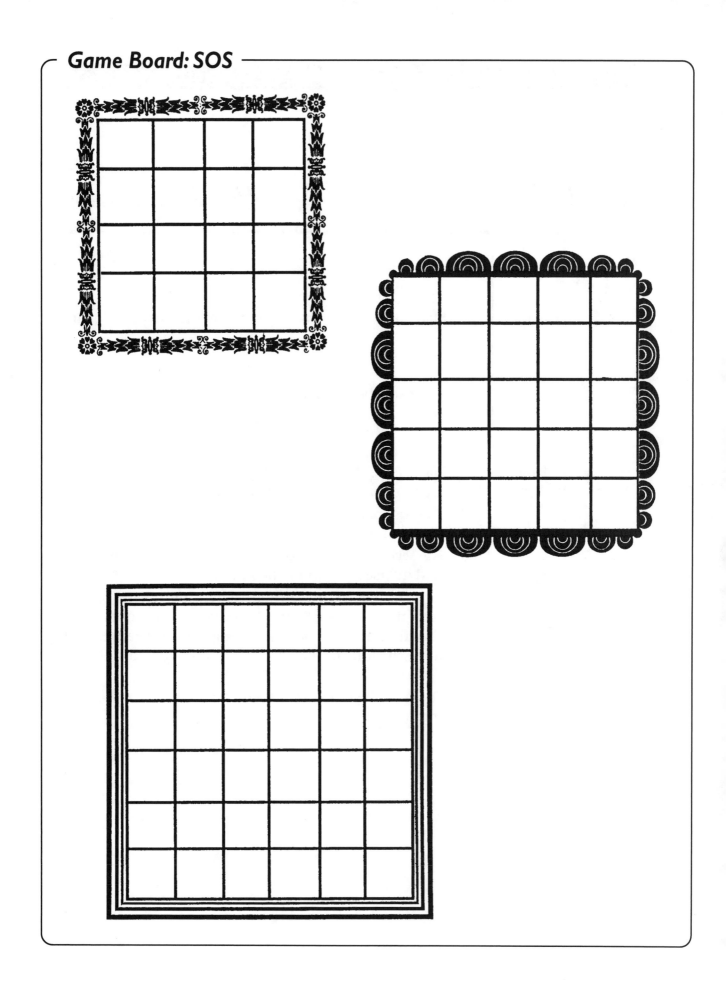

Achi

A West African game

Number of Players	2
Object	To place three game tokens in a row on the game board
Materials	copy of game board (page 13) 2 different sets of 4 game tokens each
Playing the Game	1. Players decide who will play first. After the first game, the loser of the previous game plays first. 2. The first player places a token on any empty corner or intersection of the game board. 3. The second player places a token on any other unoccupied intersection on the board. 4. In turn, players place their remaining tokens on unoccupied intersections. Once all eight tokens are placed, players move by sliding one of their tokens along the lines of the board to an unoccupied, adjacent intersection. 5. The first player to arrange three tokens in a row is the winner.

Three-Man Morris

A traditional English game

Number of Players	2
Object	To place three game tokens in a row on the game board
Materials	copy of game board (page 15) 2 different sets of 3 game tokens each
Playing the Game	1. Each player uses three tokens or "men." Players decide who will play first. After the first game, the loser of the previous game plays first.
	2. In turn, players place men at any empty corner or intersection on the game board. Only one man may occupy an intersection at one time. Players try to place 3 men in a row, forming a "mill."
	3. Once all men have been placed on the board, players take turns moving their men along the lines of the board, from one intersection to any unoccupied, adjacent one. The first player to form a mill with three tokens is the winner.

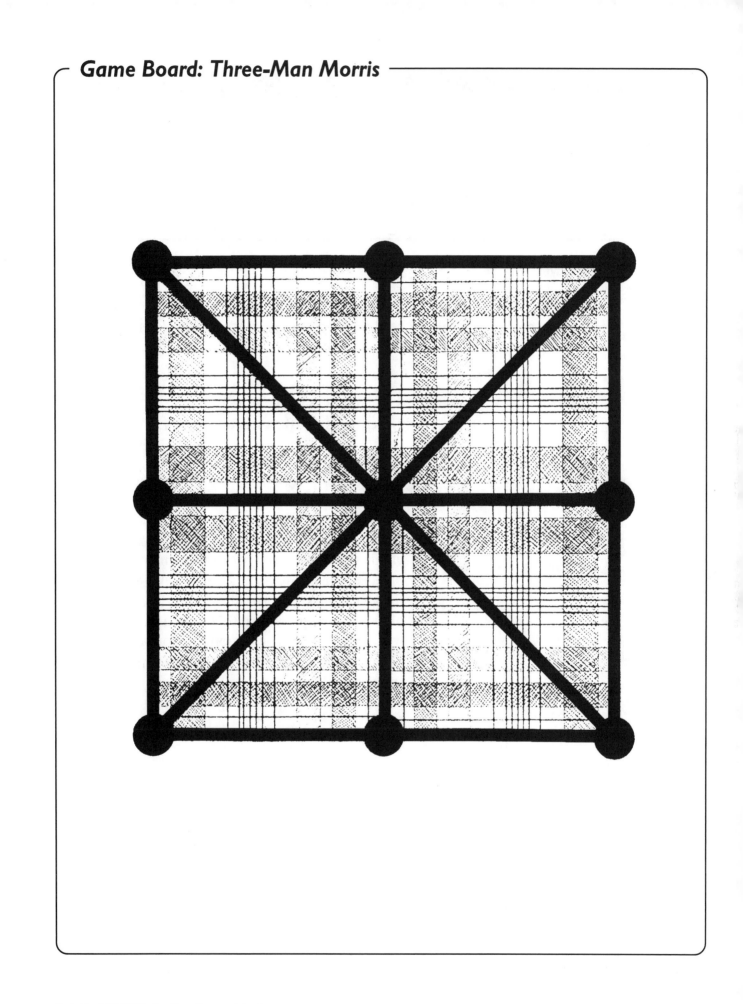

Four in a Row

Number of Players	2
Object	To be the first player to place four tokens in a row on the game board
Materials	copy of game board (page 17) 2 different sets of 18 game tokens each
Playing the Game	1. Each player selects a set of 18 markers—black and red checkers, plastic tokens, coins, or large seeds, for example.
	2. Players decide who will play first. After the first game, the loser of the previous game plays first.
	3. Players take turns placing their tokens on any unoccupied space on the game board. Each player tries to place four tokens in a straight line while preventing the opponent from doing so.
	4. The first player to place four tokens in a row is the winner.

Game Board: Four in a Row

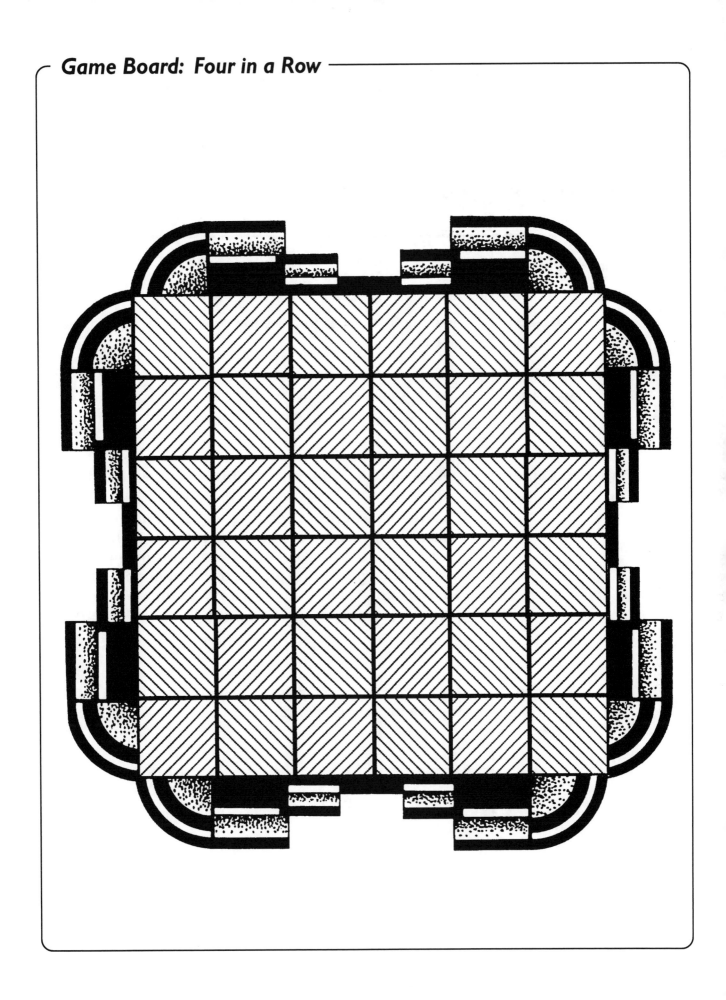

Four on Six

Number of Players	2
Object	To be the first player to place four tokens in a row on the game board
Materials	copy of game board (page 19) 2 different sets of about 20 game tokens each
Playing the Game	1. Players decide who will play first. After the first game, the loser of the previous game plays first. 2. Players take turns placing their tokens on any unoccupied hexagonal space on the game board. Each player tries to place four tokens in a straight line, in any direction, while preventing the opponent from doing so. A row of more than four tokens is *not* a win. 3. The first player to place four tokens in a row is the winner.
Variation	This game may also be played as Five on Six, with five tokens in a row being the winning move.

Game Board: Four on Six, Hexcheckers

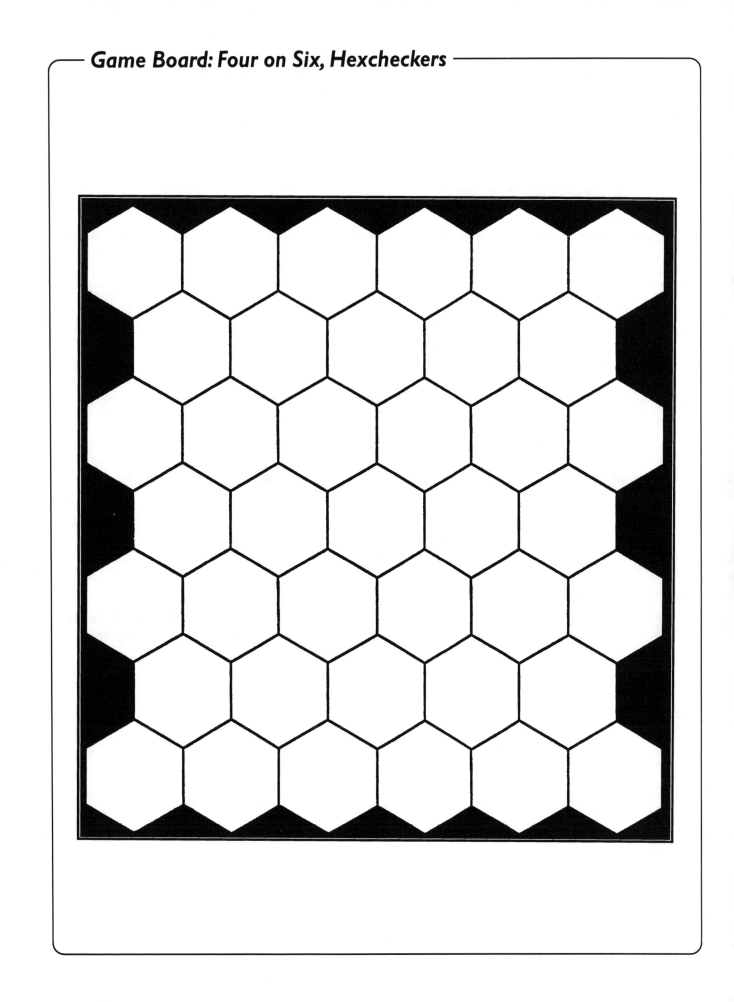

Diamonds

Number of Players	2
Object	To be the first to complete a 4-space diamond pattern on the game board
Materials	copy of game board (page 21) 2 different sets of 25 small tokens each
Playing the Game	1. Players decide who will play first. After the first game, the loser of the previous game plays first. 2. Players take turns placing their tokens on the game board. 3. The first player to place four tokens in a diamond pattern is the winner.
Variations	1. Players may continue placing tokens until all spaces on the board are filled. The player who makes the most diamonds is the winner. 2. Completing the four corners of a perfect diamond pattern of any size counts for a win, no matter how far apart those four corners are on the board.

Game Board: Diamonds

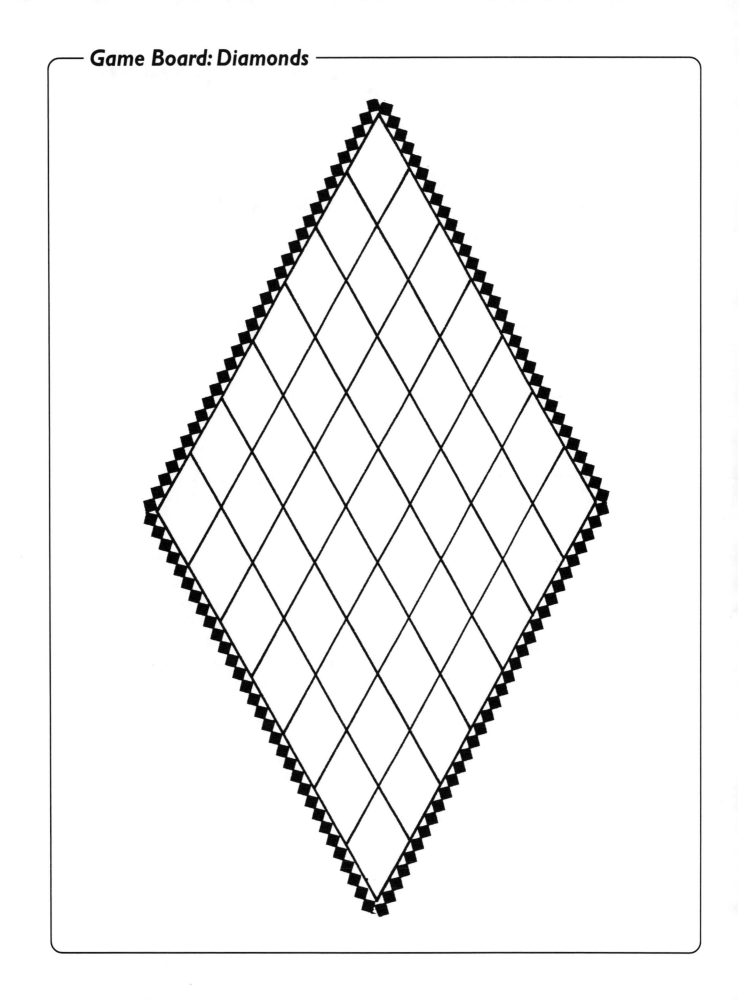

Go Moku
A traditional Japanese game

Number of Players	2
Object	To place five tokens in a row on the game board
Materials	copy of game board (page 23) 2 sets of 5 tokens each
Playing the Game	1. Players decide who will play first. After the first game, the loser of the previous game plays first.
	2. The first player places one of her tokens on any square on the game board.
	3. The second player places a token on any other square.
	4. Players continue alternating turns, placing tokens on the board. Each player tries to place five tokens in a straight line, either vertically, horizontally, or diagonally, and to prevent the opponent from doing so.
	5. The first player to place five tokens in a row is the winner. A row of 6 or more tokens is *not* a win.

Game Board: Go Moku

Hasami Shogi   *A Japanese game*

Number of Players	2
Object	To arrange five tokens in a row in any direction on the game board
Materials	copy of game board (page 26) 2 different sets of 18 tokens each

Playing the Game

1. Each player places his 18 tokens on the first two rows of squares on his side of the game board.

2. In turn, each player moves one token one square at a time, either vertically or horizontally. Tokens may not be moved diagonally.

3. Tokens may also jump over another token to an empty square immediately beyond it. Multiple jumps are allowed. Players may jump over their own tokens or their opponent's tokens. Tokens are not captured by jumping; jumping is a method of moving only.

4. A player captures an opponent's token by trapping or sandwiching it between two of his own. When a token is trapped, it is removed from the board. A player may move his own token between two of his opponent's tokens without being captured.

   A token is also captured when it is trapped in a corner between two opposing tokens in an L-shape (see figure 2 for legal traps).

5. Each player tries to complete a row of five of his own tokens in any direction—vertically, horizontally, or diagonally. Rows of five in either of the two end rows where the player's tokens began the game do not count. The first player to make a row of five is the winner.

Hasami Shogi (continued)

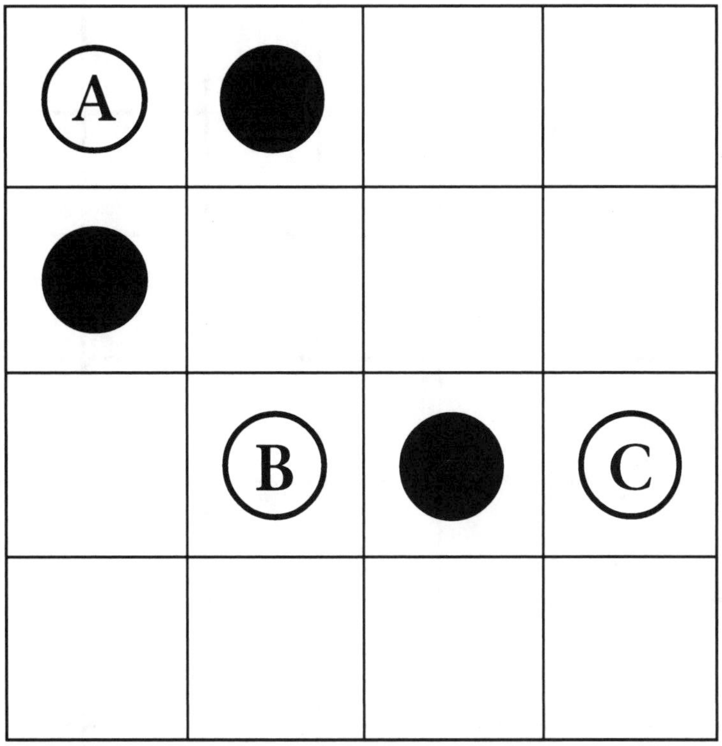

Figure 2. Example of legal traps for Hasami Shogi: Token A is trapped between the two black tokens in the corner. The other black token has been trapped between tokens B and C.

Sliders (Well Kono)

A traditional Korean game

Number of Players	2
Object	To trap an opponent so that she cannot move
Materials	copy of game board (page 28) 2 different sets of 2 game tokens each
Playing the Game	1. Players decide who will play first. After the first game, the loser of the previous game plays first. 2. The first player places one token on any intersection of the game board. 3. The second player places a token on any unoccupied intersection of the board. 4. In turn, players place their remaining tokens on unoccupied intersections. Once all four tokens are placed, players continue play by sliding one of their tokens along the lines of the game board to an adjacent, unoccupied intersection. 5. Each player attempts to trap the other so that she cannot move. The first player to trap the opponent is the winner.

Game Board: Sliders

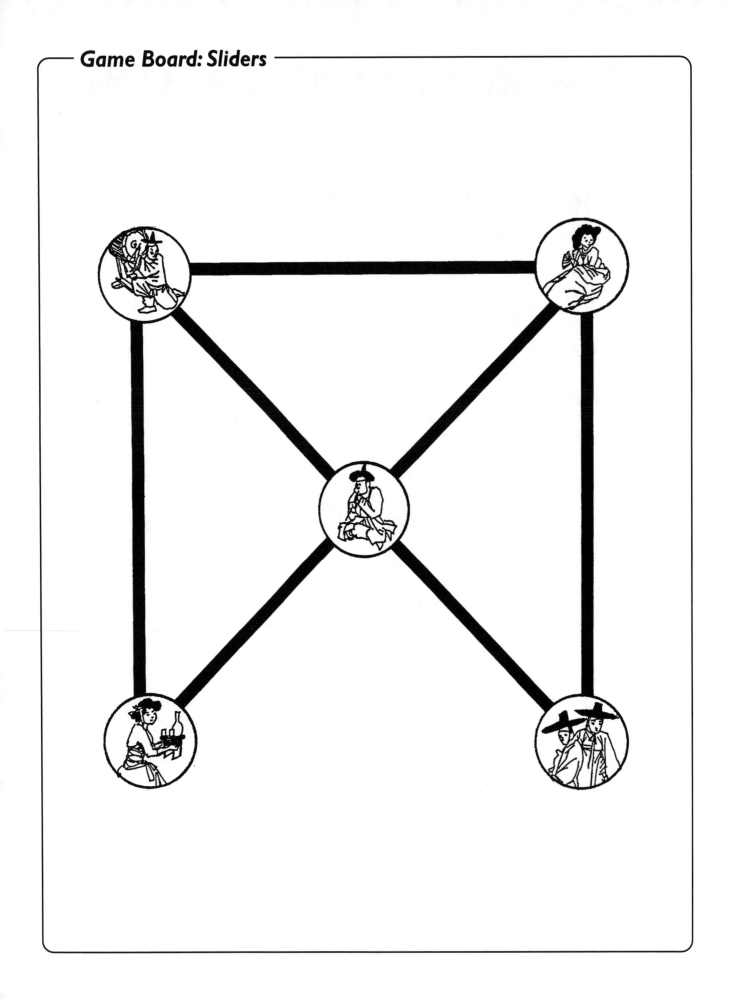

Madelinette

Number of Players	2
Object	To trap your opponent so that he cannot move
Materials	copy of game board (page 30) 2 different sets of 3 game tokens each
Playing the Game	1. Players decide who will play first. After the first game, the loser of the previous game plays first. 2. The first player places a token on any intersection of the game board. 3. The second player places a token on any unoccupied intersection of the board. 4. In turn, players place their remaining tokens on unoccupied intersections. Once all six tokens are placed, players continue play by sliding one of their tokens along the lines of the game board to an adjacent, unoccupied intersection. 5. As in Sliders, each player attempts to trap the other so that he cannot move. The first player to trap the opponent is the winner.

Source: Gyles Brandreth, *World's Best Indoor Games*, New York, Pantheon Books, 1981. Used with permission.

Mu-Torere

A traditional Maori game

Number of Players	2
Object	To block the opponent from moving
Materials	copy of game board (page 32) 2 different sets of 4 tokens each
Playing the Game	

1. The center position on the game board is called the *putahi*. The positions at the end of each ray of the eight-pointed star are called *kewai*. Tokens may be moved along the lines to an adjacent, unoccupied position—either the putahi or one of the kewai.

2. One player places four tokens on four adjacent kewai on one side of the board. The other player places tokens on the other four adjacent kewai.

3. Players decide who will play first. After the first game, the loser of the previous game plays first.

4. The first player moves one of her tokens to the putahi. However, on this first move only, the player may not move a token so that the second player is unable to move.

5. Players take turns moving one of their tokens to the empty position on the board, either the putahi or any adjacent kewai, until one player blocks the other from moving. That player is the winner.

Game Board: Mu-Torere

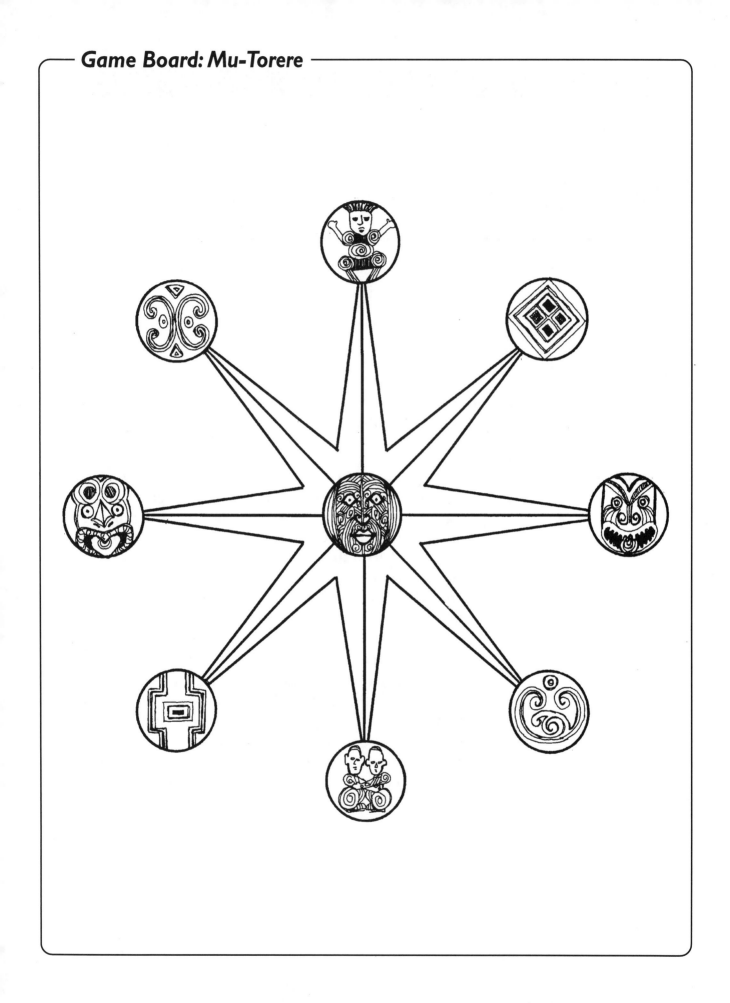

Fox and Hounds

A traditional English game

Number of Players	2
Object	For the hounds: to trap the fox in space 1; for the fox: to escape to space 11
Materials	copy of game board (page 34) 1 fox token and 3 hound tokens
Playing the Game	1. Players decide who will play the fox and who will play the hounds. Place the fox token on space 1. Place the three hounds' tokens on spaces 8, 10 and 11. The fox moves first.

1. Players decide who will play the fox and who will play the hounds. Place the fox token on space 1. Place the three hounds' tokens on spaces 8, 10 and 11. The fox moves first.
2. Tokens may be moved only to an adjacent, unoccupied space along the lines of the board. Tokens may not jump over empty spaces or other tokens.
3. Hounds may move only up, down, forward (to the left), or diagonally forward. They may not move backward (to the right) or diagonally backward. The fox may move in any direction.
4. The hounds win if they trap the fox in space 1. The fox wins if he can get past the hounds to reach space 11. The fox also wins if there is a stalemate (repeated moves back and forth).
5. Players switch roles after each game. The first player to win two games in a row—one as the fox and one as the hounds—wins the match.

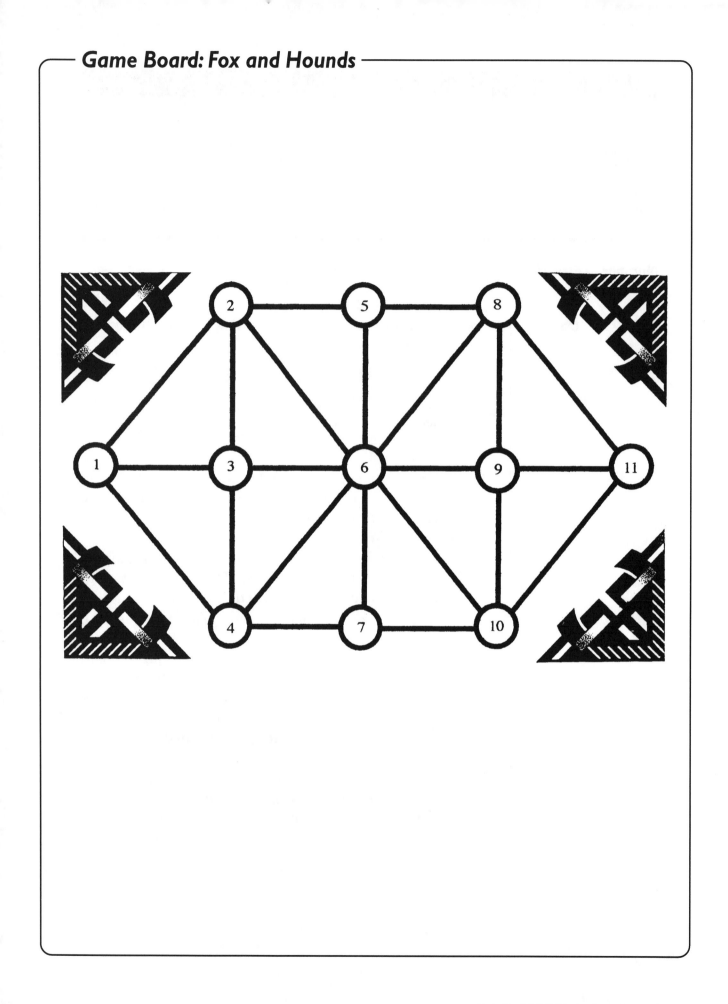

Cop and Robber

Number of Players	2
Object	For the cop: to catch the robber within 25 moves; for the robber: to avoid being caught
Materials	copy of game board (page 36) 2 different tokens
Playing the Game	

1. Players decide who will play the cop and who will play the robber. White pathways on the game board represent streets, and gray squares represent city blocks.
2. The cop moves first by placing his token on any street intersection on the board except one of the four center intersections.
3. The robber then places his token on any other intersection of the board.
4. The cop moves first. Players take turns moving by sliding tokens along the white roadways to adjacent intersections one block away. Players may move in any direction—north, south, east, or west.
5. If the cop lands on the intersection already occupied by the robber within 25 moves, he wins. If the robber manages to avoid the cop for 25 moves, he wins.
6. After each game, players reverse roles. The first player to win two games in a row—one as the cop and one as the robber—wins the match.

Source: *The Big Book of Puzzles,* Michael Holt and Ronald Ridout, Longman Group Ltd., London, 1972. Used with permission.

Game Board: Cop and Robber

Checkerboard Fox and Geese

Number of Players	2
Object	For the geese: to trap the fox; for the fox: to escape the geese's trap
Materials	copy of game board (page 38) 4 black checkers and 1 red checker
Playing the Game	1. Players decide who will play the fox and who will play the geese. Place the geese (black checkers) on the four black squares of the last row on one side of the checkerboard. The fox (the red checker) may be placed on any of the black squares of the last row on the opposite side of the board.

2. Play is on the black squares only. Geese move first. The person playing the geese may move any one checker diagonally forward one square at a time. Geese may not move backward. The geese attempt to trap the fox in a corner so he cannot move. When that happens, the geese have won.

3. The fox may move one square at a time, either forward or backward. The fox attempts to break through the line of geese. If he does so, the fox wins.

4. Players continue alternating turns until one or the other has won. Players then switch roles for the next game. The first player to win two games in a row wins the match.

Game Board: Checkerboard Fox and Geese

Six-Man Morris

A traditional English game

Number of Players	2
Object	To prevent your opponent from making a move, or to capture four of his men
Materials	copy of game board (page 40) 2 sets of 6 different game tokens each
Playing the Game	1. Each player uses six tokens or "men." Players decide who will play first. After the first game, the loser of the previous game plays first.
	2. In turn, players place men at any empty corner or intersection on the game board. Only one man may occupy an intersection at a time. Players try to place 3 men in a row, forming a "mill."
	3. When a player forms a mill, he removes one of the opponent's pieces from the board. The player may remove any opposing piece that is not currently part of a mill. However, if all opposing pieces are currently in mills, the player may remove any one of those pieces from the board. Once a token is removed, it may no longer be used in the game.
	4. Once all men have been placed on the board, players take turns moving their men from one intersection to any adjacent, unoccupied one. Players continue forming mills and removing men.
	5. The game is over when one player has only two men remaining, or when a player blocks the opponent so he cannot make a move. The player who has captured four of the opponent's men or blocked all his moves is the winner.

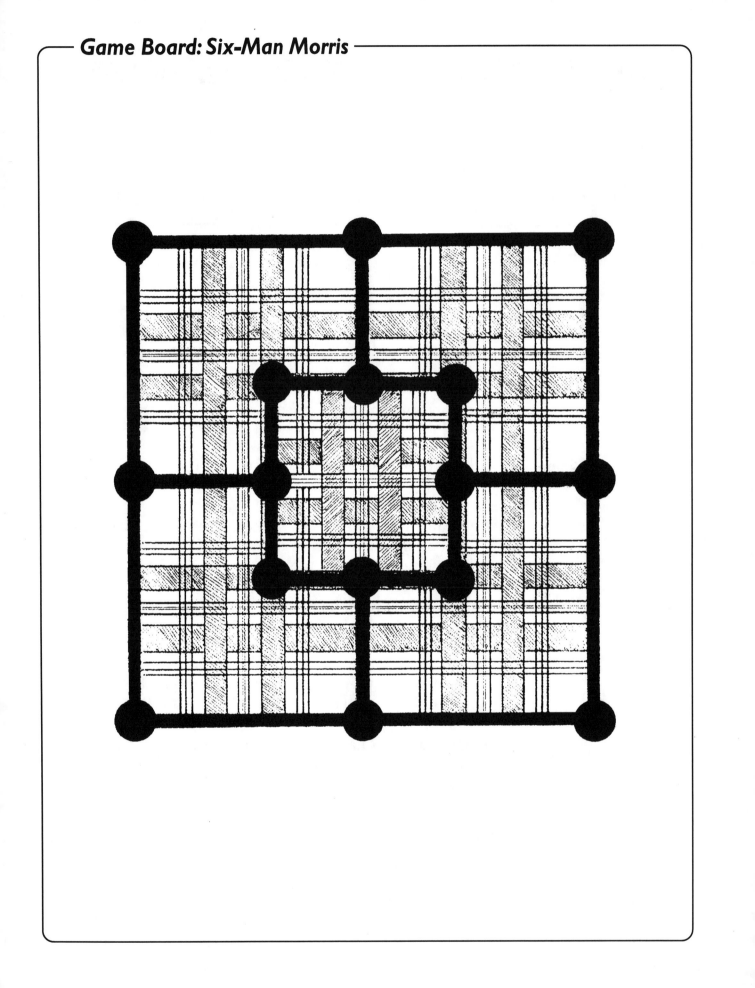

Nine-Man Morris

A traditional English game

Number of Players	2
Object	To prevent your opponent from making a move, or to capture seven of her men
Materials	copy of game board (page 42) 2 different sets of 9 game tokens each
Playing the Game	1. Each player uses nine tokens or "men." Players decide who will play first. After the first game, the loser of the previous game plays first.
	2. In turn, players place men at any empty intersection on the game board. Only one man may occupy any spot at a time. Players try to place 3 men in a row, forming a "mill."
	3. When a player forms a mill, she removes one of her opponent's pieces from the board. The player may remove any opposing piece that is not currently part of a mill. If all opposing pieces are currently in mills, the player may remove one of those pieces from the board. Once a token is removed, it may no longer be used in the game.
	4. Once all men have been placed on the board, players take turns moving their men from one intersection to any adjacent, unoccupied one. Players continue forming mills and removing men.
	5. The game is over when one player has only two men remaining, or when a player blocks the opponent so she cannot move. The player who has captured seven of the opponent's men or blocked all his moves is the winner.

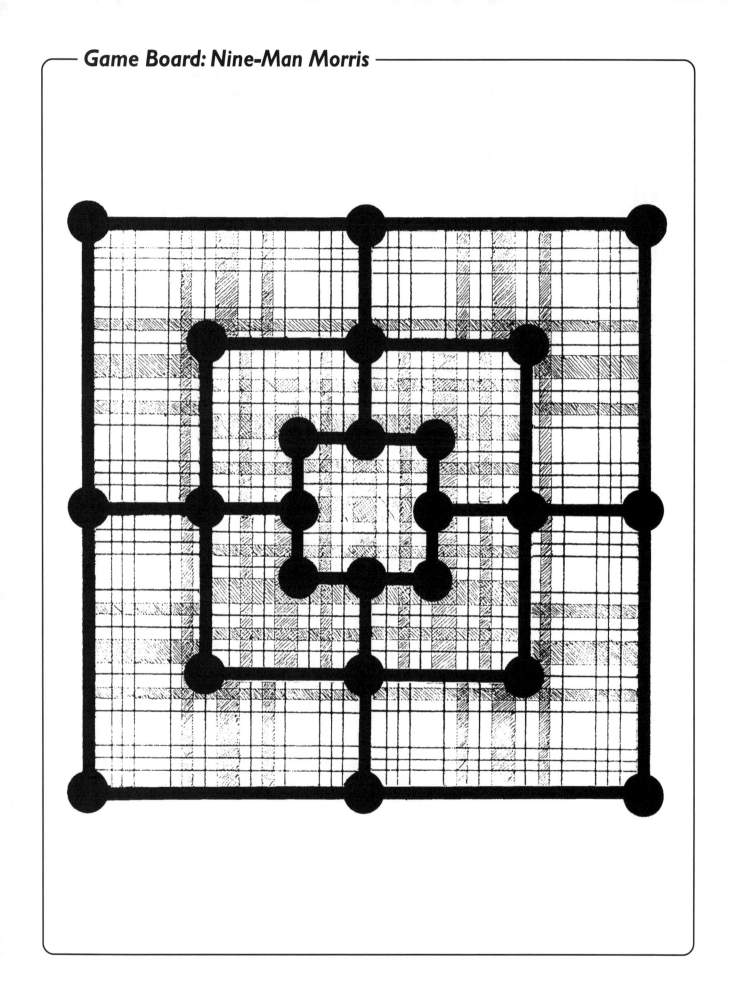

Octotrap

Number of Players	2
Object	To trap the most octagons by surrounding them with four squares
Materials	copy of game board (page 44) 2 different sets of 24 tokens each
Playing the Game	1. Players decide who will play first. After the first game, the loser of the previous game plays first.
	2. Players take turns placing their tokens on the small squares on the game board. Each player attempts to capture octagons by surrounding them with tokens.
	3. When a player captures an octagon, he places a token in the octagon to claim it. A player who traps an octagon also gets an extra turn, and may place another token in any empty square.
	4. The game is over when it is no longer possible for either player to trap any more octagons. The player who has captured the most octagons is the winner.

Game Board: Octotrap

Coyote and Chickens (Fox and Geese)

Number of Players	2
Object	Coyote: To jump and "eat" at least 12 chickens; chickens: to trap the coyote so she cannot move
Materials	copy of game board (page 46) 12 "chicken" tokens and 1 "coyote" token

Playing the Game

1. Players decide who will play Coyote and who will play the chickens. Players alternate roles in the games that follow. The coyote token is placed on the center intersection of the board. The 12 chicken tokens are placed on the other intersections marked with black dots.

2. Coyote moves first. Coyote may move 1 space in any direction, vertically, horizontally, or diagonally. She captures and eats a chicken by jumping over it onto an empty space immediately beyond it. Multiple jumps are allowed. When a chicken is eaten, it is removed from the board.

3. The chickens move second. Only one chicken may move per turn. Chickens may move either sideways or forward. They may not move diagonally or backward. Chickens do not jump.

4. Players continue alternating turns until Coyote has eaten 7 chickens, or until the chickens have trapped Coyote so that she cannot move.

5. Players then reverse roles to play the next game. The player who wins two games in a row—one as Coyote and one as the chickens—wins the match.

Variation

The game may also be played with no limitation on the direction that chickens may move. All other rules remain the same.

Game Board: Coyote and Chickens

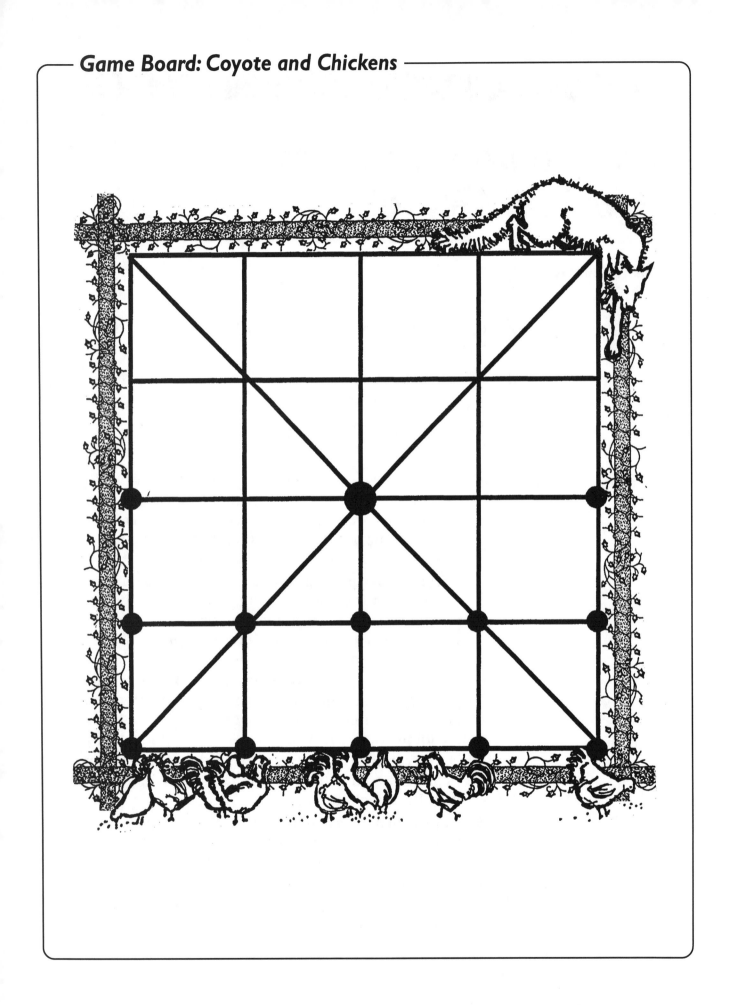

Cows and Leopards

A traditional Sri Lankan game

Number of Players	2
Object	Leopards: to eat the cows by jumping them; cows: to trap the leopards so they cannot move
Materials	copy of game board (page 48) 24 cow tokens; 2 leopard tokens

Playing the Game

1. Players decide who will play the cows and who will play the leopards. Roles are exchanged after each game.

2. The person playing the leopards places one leopard token on the center intersection of the game board.

3. The other player then places a cow token on any other intersection of the board.

4. The first player then places the second leopard on any other vacant intersection on the board.

5. Players take turns. The second player must place all 24 cows on the board before he may move any of them. The first player may begin moving since both leopards are on the board.

6. Leopards may move along any line on the board, in any direction, to an adjacent empty intersection. Leopards may also "eat" a cow by jumping over it to an empty intersection immediately beyond the cow. The jumped cow is removed from the board. A leopard must take a jump if it is available to him. Multiple jumps are allowed.

7. Cows may move along any line on the board, in any direction, to an adjacent empty intersection on the board. Cows may not jump.

8. Play continues until both leopards are trapped so that they cannot move, or until the leopards have eaten enough cows (10 or more) that they cannot be trapped.

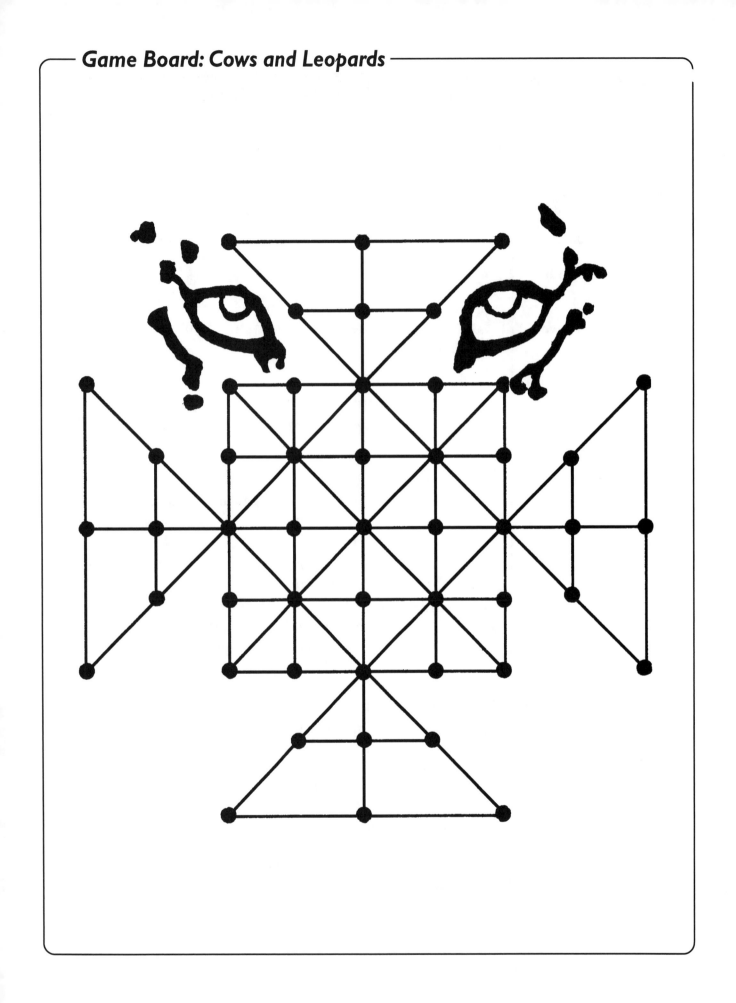

Reversi

Number of Players	2
Object	To score the most points by "trapping" and reversing game tokens
Materials	checkerboard or copy of game board (page 51)
	64 pennies (or larger coins) or other tokens with two clearly different sides

Playing the Game

1. Players decide who will play first. After the first game, the loser of the previous game plays first. They also decide who will play "heads" and who will play "tails."

2. Play starts with four coins or tokens in the four center squares of the checkerboard or grid. Two coins must show heads, and the other two must show tails.

3. Let's suppose the first player is playing heads. He places another coin, heads up, on a square of the board adjacent to the coins already in place. His move must trap one or more coins showing tails in a direct line (vertical, horizontal, or diagonal) between two coins showing heads. The player then flips any trapped coins so they also show heads.

4. The second player then places a coin on the board, tails up. This move must trap at least one of her opponent's coins between two of her own. She then flips the coins she has trapped to show tails.

5. Players continue to take turns putting down tokens. A player must flip at least one of her opponents tokens on each move. Often, a player will be able to flip several tokens, sometimes in several different directions. There is no limit to the number of times during the game that a coin may be flipped.

Reversi (continued)

6. A player may flip coins that are trapped only as a direct result of the current move. As he flips coins, others showing the opposite face may appear to become trapped. But those traps are not a direct result of the player's current move and should not be reversed.

7. The game is over when a player can't make any move to flip at least one coin. Players then count the number of coins on the board showing their side. The player with the largest number of coins is the winner.

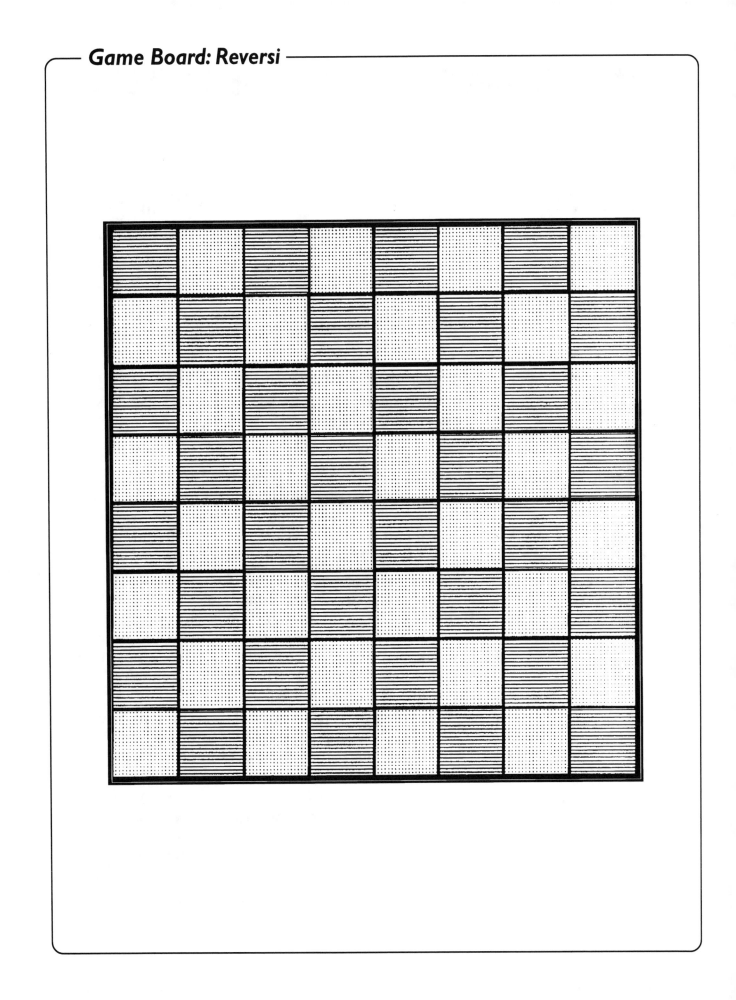

Derrah

A North African game

Number of Players	2
Object	To form vertical or horizontal rows of three tokens
Materials	copy of game board (page 53) 2 different sets of 12 tokens each (a set of black and red checkers, for example)
Playing the Game	1. Players decide who will play first. After the first game, the loser of the previous game plays first. 2. Players take turns placing their tokens on any empty square on the game board. This continues until all 24 tokens have been placed on the board. 3. Players take turns moving any token from one square on the board to any adjacent, unoccupied square, trying to arrange three (and only three) of their tokens in either vertical or horizontal rows. Rows of three that were made while players were placing their tokens do not count. Tokens may be moved vertically or horizontally. Diagonal moves are not allowed. 4. Each time players make a row of three, they may remove any one of the opponent's tokens from the board. Making a row longer than three does not allow a player to remove an opposing token. 5. Moving a token away from a row of three on one move, and then reforming the same row of three on the following move is permitted. As in step 4, remaking the row of three allows the player to remove another of the opponent's pieces. 6. The first player to capture ten of the opponent's tokens is the winner.

Game Board: Derrah

Shogi

A Japanese game

Number of Players	2
Object	To remove opponent's tokens from the board by trapping them
Materials	game board (page 26) 2 different sets of 9 tokens each

Playing the Game

1. Each player places his nine tokens on the first row of nine squares on his side of the game board.

2. In turn, each player moves one token. Tokens may be moved 1 square in any direction—forward, backward, or sideways.

3. Tokens may also jump over another token to an empty square immediately beyond it. Multiple jumps are allowed. Players may jump over their own tokens or their opponent's. Tokens are not captured by jumping. Jumping is a method of moving only.

4. A player captures an opponent's token by trapping it between two of his own. When a token is trapped, it is removed from the board. A token is also captured if it is trapped in an L-shape between two opposing tokens in a corner of the board (see figure 2 page 25 for legal traps).

5. A player may move his own token between two of his opponent's tokens without being captured.

6. The first player to capture eight of the opponent's tokens is the winner.

Source: *The World Book of Children's Games,* by Arnold Arnold. Used with permission.

Seega

A traditional African game

Number of Players	2
Object	To remove all opponent's men from the game board or have more men left on the board at the end of play
Materials	copy of game board (page 56) 2 different sets of 12 tokens each
Playing the Game	

1. Players decide who will begin. After the first game, the player who won the previous game plays first.

2. Players take turns placing tokens on any squares of the game board except the center one. Each player places two tokens on the board during her turn. After all the tokens are on the board, the player who placed the final two tokens makes the first move. If this player cannot make a move, she removes any one of her opponent's pieces from the board as her first turn. It is then the second player's turn to move.

3. Players move by sliding one of their tokens either vertically or horizontally to an empty square. Tokens may not be moved diagonally. Each player tries to trap, or sandwich, one of her opponent's tokens between two of her own. The trapped token is removed from the board.

4. If a player's move results in a capture, that player may move that same token again, if and only if the next move results in another capture.

5. If a single move results in two traps of two of the opponent's tokens at the same time, both the trapped tokens are removed from the board.

6. A player may move her own token in between two opponent's tokens without losing it.

7. The player who captures all her opponent's pieces is the winner. In case neither player may move, the player with the most tokens remaining on the board is the winner.

Dama or Turkish Checkers

Number of Players	2
Object	To capture or block all your opponent's men
Materials	game board (page 59) or standard checkerboard 2 sets of 16 tokens each (known as "men")
Playing the Game	1. The board is set up as shown in the diagram below. Players decide who will play first. After the first game, the loser of the previous game goes first.

O = open square—X,Y = players' men

```
O O O O O O O O
X X X X X X X X
X X X X X X X X
O O O O O O O O
O O O O O O O O
Y Y Y Y Y Y Y Y
Y Y Y Y Y Y Y Y
O O O O O O O O
```

2. In turn, each player moves a man one space forward or one space sideways to an open square on the board. No backward or diagonal moves are allowed.

3. A player captures an opponent's man by jumping over it to an empty square immediately beyond it, as in checkers. Multiple jumps are permitted. Men may jump and capture either forward or sideways, but not diagonally. The captured token is removed from the board.

Dama or Turkish Checkers (continued)

Playing the Game

4. If an opponent's man can be taken, it must be taken. If a player fails to make a capturing move, the opponent may remove the man that could have made the capture from the board before making his next move. This rule applies to both ordinary men and to kings.

5. A man that reaches the home row on the opponent's side of the board becomes a king. Kings should be "crowned" by stacking a second token on top, as in ordinary checkers. Kings may move in a straight line across all empty spaces that are in that line. Kings may move forward, backward, or sideways. They may not move diagonally. Kings capture in any direction by landing on an empty square immediately beyond an opponent's man. Kings may also make multiple jumps.

6. The player who captures all his opponent's men or who blocks his opponent from making any further moves is the winner.

Game Board: Dama or Turkish Checkers (and other games)

Diagonal Checkers

Number of Players	2
Object	To capture all opponent's men
Materials	game board (page 59) or checkerboard 2 sets of 16 tokens each

Playing the Game

1. Turn the checkerboard so that each player sits at a corner with a white square. Place 12 black and 12 red checkers on the black squares, leaving the center line of black squares empty. Before play begins, players must decide whether or not they will play with "flying kings"—kings that may move an unlimited number of spaces in any one direction on a single move.

2. Play follows all the rules of ordinary checkers. Checkers may move on the black squares only. They may move sideways or forward, but not backward. Men are promoted to kings only on the two black squares in the corner opposite from where the player begins her attack. Kings may move backward as well as forward or sideways.

3. The player who captures all her opponent's men is the winner.

Variation

Start the game with the board turned so that each player sits at a corner with a shaded square. In this version, each player starts with only nine men, and the two center lines of black squares are left open. A man is promoted to king only after it reaches the one corner square.

Giveaway or Backward Checkers

Number of Players | 2

Object | To be the first person to lose all checkers

Materials | game board (page 59) or standard checkerboard
2 sets of 16 tokens each

Playing the Game

1. Set up the board as you would for an ordinary checker game.
2. All rules of ordinary checkers apply. Jumps, including multiple jumps, must be taken when they are available.
3. As in ordinary checkers, when a man reaches the farthest row, it is crowned a king and may then move or jump one square in any direction, backward or forward. Do not use "flying kings"—kings that may move any number of squares in a straight line on a single turn—in the game of Giveaway.
4. Each player attempts to force the other to take his men as quickly as possible. The first player to lose all his checkers is the winner.

Liberian Checkers

Number of Players	2
Object	To be the last player with tokens left on the board
Materials	copy of game board (page 64) 2 sets of 10 tokens each
Playing the Game	1. Each player places four tokens on the board as shown in figure 3. Players decide who will play first. After the first game, the loser of the previous game plays first.

STARTING PLAY

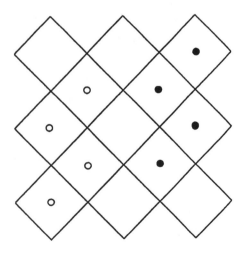

LEGAL MOVES

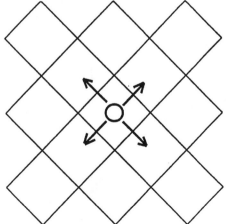

Figure 3. Moves for Liberian Checkers

Liberian Checkers (continued)

ILLEGAL MOVES

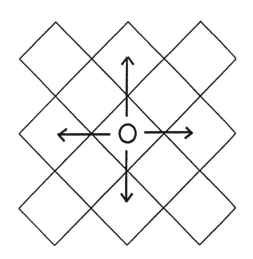

Figure 3. Moves for Liberian Checkers *(continued)*

2. A token may move onto any empty square directly beside it, in any direction. A player captures an opponent's token by jumping over it onto a vacant square immediately beyond it, as in checkers. However, tokens may not move or jump across the corners of the squares, as they would on an ordinary checkerboard (see figure 3).

3. Jumps, including multiple jumps, must be taken when they are available.

4. When a player loses a token, she replaces it from her store of remaining tokens. The player may place the new piece on any vacant square on the board. This replacement counts as the player's turn, and her opponent then has the next move. Once there are no more tokens remaining in the store, players continue play with tokens remaining on the board.

5. If a player repeats the same move back and forth between two squares three times in a row in order to avoid capture, she forfeits the game.

6. Play continues until one player has lost all her tokens. The player with tokens remaining is the winner.

Based on an African game board from *A History of Board Games Other Than Chess* by H. J. R. Murray, Oxford University Press, 1952.

Game Board: Liberian Checkers

Alquerque

An ancient North African game,
later brought to Spain and then to the Americas

Number of Players

2

Object

To capture all opponent's men or block them from moving

Materials

copy of game board (page 66)
2 different sets of 12 tokens each

Playing the Game

1. Players arrange their men on the black dots of the game board, leaving the center position open, as shown below.

   X X X X X
   X X X X X
   X X   O O
   O O O O O
   O O O O O

2. Players take turns moving one of their tokens to any empty intersection on the board. Tokens may be moved forward, sideways, or diagonally, but not backward.

3. Players capture opponent's men as in checkers, by jumping over them to an empty intersection immediately beyond. Multiple jumps are allowed. Tokens may not jump backward.

4. If an opponent's man can be taken, it must be taken. If a player fails to take a jump, his opponent may remove that token from the board, as in checkers.

5. Once a token has reached the farthest row on the opponent's side of the board, it may not move, unless it can jump one or more of the opponent's men.

6. A player wins by capturing all opponent's men, or by blocking his opponent so that none of his men may move. The game is a draw if an equal number of men have reached the farthest row of the board, or if both players are blocked so that neither one can move.

Game Board: Alquerque

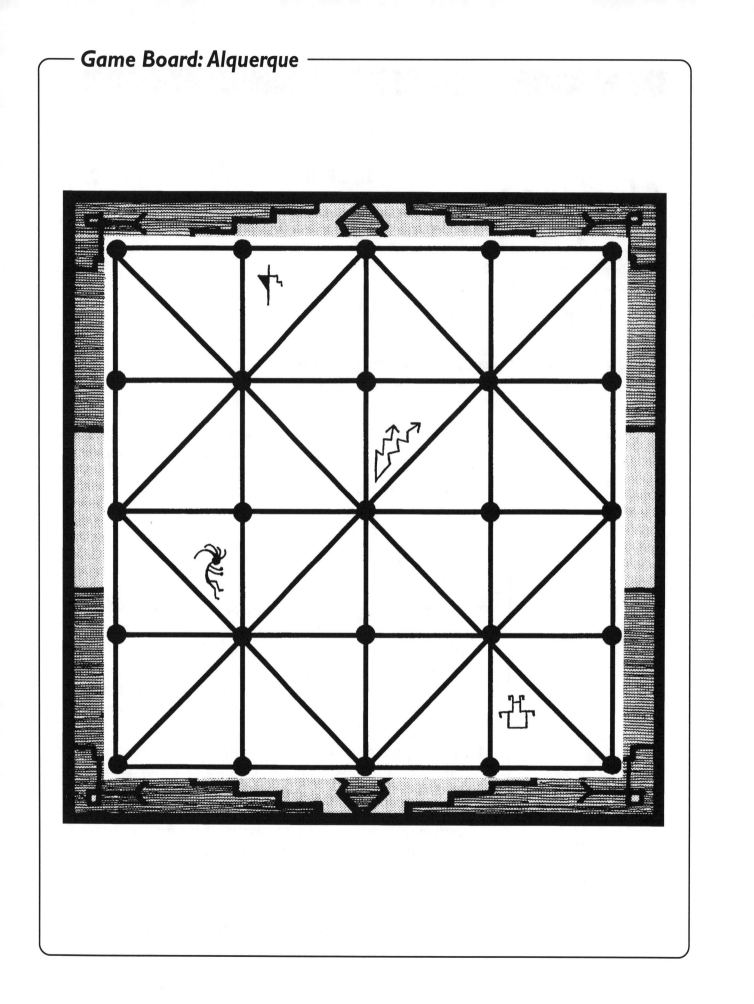

Fighting Serpents

A Zuni variation of Alquerque

Number of Players	2
Object	To capture all opponent's tokens
Materials	copy of game board (page 68) 2 sets of 23 tokens each
Playing the Game	1. Players place their tokens on the game board as shown, leaving the center intersection and the two end intersections empty.

x x x x x x x x x x x x x x x

o o o o o o   x x x x x x

o o o o o o o o o o o o o o o

2. Players decide who will play first. After the first game, the loser of the previous game plays first. On each move, a player may move any one of her tokens to any empty, adjacent intersection.

3. Players capture opposing tokens by jumping over them to an empty intersection immediately beyond. When an opponent's token is jumped, it is removed from the board. Multiple jumps are allowed. If a jump is available, it must be taken.

4. Players may not jump and capture an opponent's token when it is on either of the intersections at the end of the board.

5. The first player to capture all the opponent's tokens is the winner.

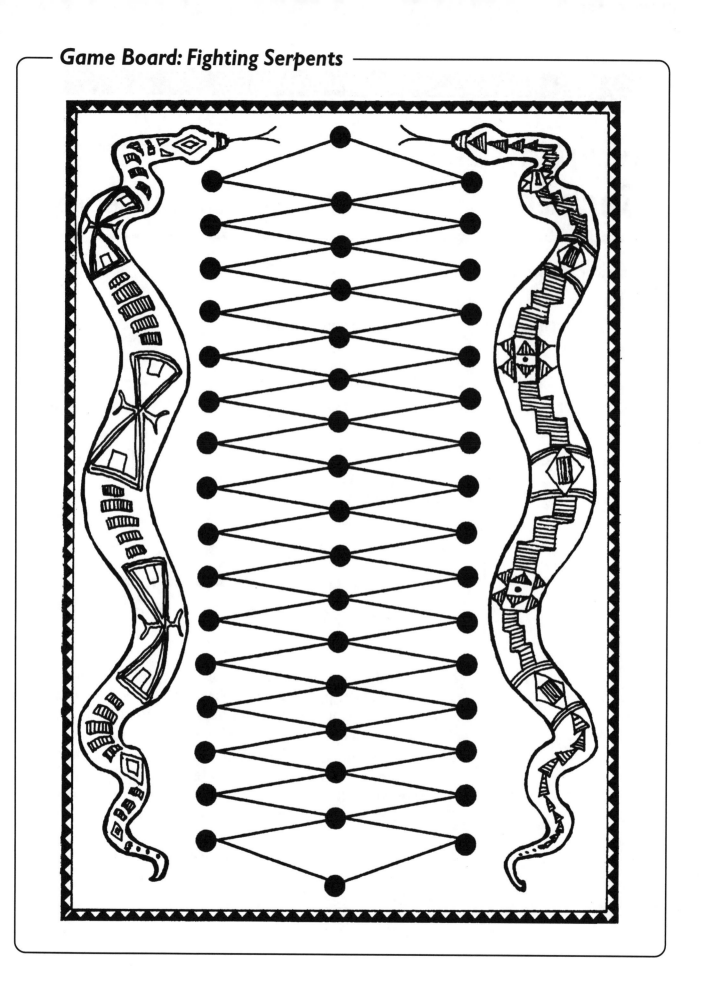

Hexcheckers

Number of Players	2
Object	To capture all opponent's men
Materials	copy of game board (page 19) 2 different sets of 12 checkers or other tokens each
Playing the Game	1. Players decide who will play first. After the first game, the loser of the previous game plays first. 2. Each player places his 12 playing pieces (men) on the game board on the 12 spaces marked with dots in figure 4.

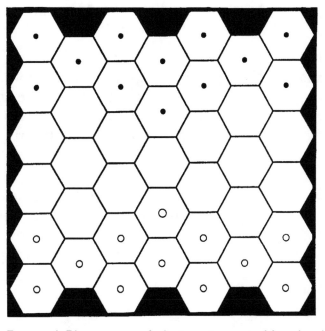

Figure 4. Placement of playing pieces in Hexcheckers

Hexcheckers (continued)

Playing the Game

3. Men may move either directly forward or diagonally forward. They may not move backward or diagonally backward.

4. Men are captured by jumping, as in checkers. Jumps must be made in a straight line. Jumps may be made only over a single man, from the space immediately in front of that man to the empty space immediately beyond it. Multiple jumps are permitted. If an opponent's man may be taken, it must be taken. If a player has a capturing move available and fails to take it, the opponent may remove the man that could have made the capture from the board before making the next move. This rule applies to both ordinary men and to kings.

5. When a man reaches one of the four spaces at the opponent's end of the board, it is crowned king with a token or checker. Kings move one space in any direction. Kings capture opposing pieces as in rule 4, except they are permitted to capture in either direction, backward or forward.

Variations

1. Flying Kings: Instead of allowing kings to move only a single space per turn, players may agree before play begins to allow kings to move as far along a straight line as possible on any turn. If this rule is used, a king making a capture must land on the space immediately beyond the man it captures.

2. Jumpers: Players may agree before play begins to allow a man to jump over another one of his own men. Ordinary men may only jump forward or diagonally forward. Kings may jump in any direction.

Extinction Chess

Number of Players	2
Object	To force one of your opponent's "species" of chessmen into extinction
Materials	copy of game board (page 59) or standard chess board standard chess pieces
Playing the Game	

1. Players decide who will play first. After the first game, the loser of the previous game plays first. All the standard moves and rules of chess apply. However, players should think of each different kind of piece—king, queen, rook, bishop, knight, and pawn—as a separate species.

2. Play proceeds as in ordinary chess. Pawns may be promoted to any other pieces, including kings, if they reach the farthest row on the board.

3. When a player loses all of any one species, the game has been lost. If, for example, a player loses both knights, she has lost the game. The same is true if a player loses both bishops, both rooks, the king, the queen, or all eight pawns.

Source: R. Wayne Schmittberger, *New Rules for Classic Games*. Used with permission.

Chinese Knights

Number of Players	2 or 4
Object	To move all playing tokens across the board to the opposite corner
Materials	copy of game board (page 59) or standard chess board 4 different sets of 6 playing tokens each
Playing the Game	1. Players turn the chess board so that each player sits at a corner. Each player places his 6 tokens on the 6 corner squares of the board, both shaded and clear. 2. Each token moves as a knight moves in chess—in an L shape. That is, it may move one square forward and two squares left or right, or one square left or right and two squares forward. Pieces may jump over other pieces, but they may not land on a square that is already occupied. 3. Players decide who will move first. In the 4-player game, play moves clockwise around the board. 4. The first player moves one of his pieces toward the opposite corner, using a knight's move only. Each player in turn continues moving pieces across the board to the opposite corner. 5. Whenever a player's token lands on one of the four central squares of the game board, the player gets another turn. On that extra turn, the player may move any of his six tokens. 6. If a player's tokens are all blocked so he cannot move, that player must pass, and the next player continues the game. 7. The player who gets all his tokens to the opposite corner first wins the game.

Queen's Command

Number of Players	2 to 4
Object	To place queens on a chess board so that no other queen on the board may capture them
Materials	copy of game board (page 59) or standard chess board different sets of several tokens each to serve as queens for each player
Playing the Game	1. Each token represents a queen. Queens may move an unlimited number of spaces on the chessboard in either a diagonal, vertical, or horizontal straight line. 2. Players decide who will play first. After the first game, the loser of the previous game plays first. The first player places a token anywhere on the chessboard. 3. The next player places her token on the board on any square where it cannot be captured by the queen already on the board. 4. Each player in turn places another queen where it can't be captured by any other queen already in play. 5. Play continues until one player can't find any safe place to put her queen. The player who made the last safe move is the winner.
Variation	This same game may also be played with knights, bishops, or rooks. Each presents its own special set of challenges.

Crucible

Number of Players	2
Object	To be the first player to connect an unbroken path from one side of the board to the other
Materials	copies of game board (page 75) pencils or pens
Playing the Game	1. Players decide who will play first, and who will play horizontally (crosses) and who will play vertically (circles). After the first game, the loser of the previous game plays first.
	2. The player choosing circles attempts to complete an unbroken path between circles from top to bottom of the game board. Meanwhile, the other player tries to complete an unbroken path between crosses from side to side. Each player tries to block the opponent while completing his own path.
	3. In turn, each player draws a vertical or horizontal line between any two of his adjacent marks. The circle player connects circles; the crosses player connects crosses. A player's move need not be connected to his previous one. Nor are players required to start at one side of the board.
	4. A player may not draw a line that crosses another line. Paths are allowed to zigzag across the board.
	5. The first player to complete an unbroken path across the entire game board is the winner.

Game Board: Crucible

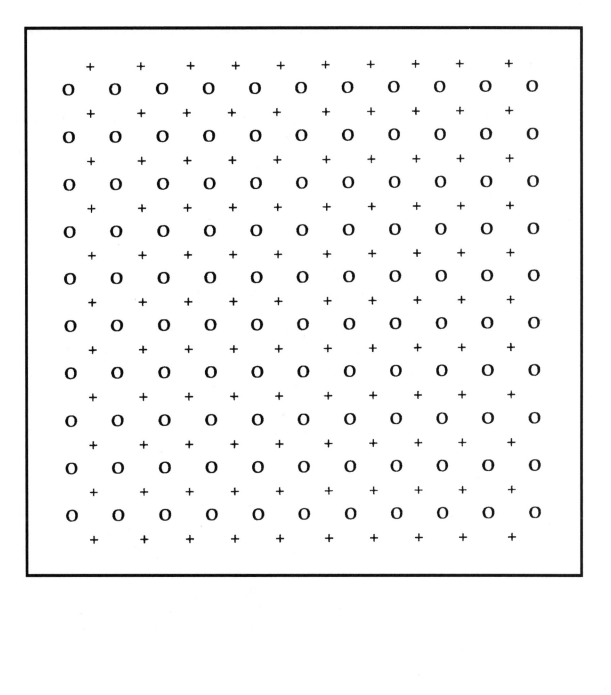

Alphamazement

Number of Players	2
Object	To be the last player to draw an unbroken line between two consecutive letters of the alphabet
Materials	copies of game board (page 77) pencils or pens

Playing the Game

1. Using pen or pencil, players take turns writing a letter of the alphabet in any 1 of the 26 squares on the game board. The letters should be scattered at random around the board and spaced well apart.

2. The first player draws a line that connects any letter with the letter that comes either before or after it in the alphabet. The line must travel through the squares on the game board either vertically or horizontally. Zigzagging is permitted—a player may use any number of right angle turns in drawing the line.

3. The second player then connects any letter with either of its neighbors in the alphabet in the same manner. If the first player connected *S* to *T,* for example, the second player may connect the *R* to the *S* or the *T* to the *U,* or the second player could connect any other two consecutive letters elsewhere in the alphabet.

4. Connecting lines may not pass through any square that contains a letter. Connecting lines may not cross other connecting lines. Once a line has passed through a square, no other line may be drawn through that square.

5. Each line is drawn lightly at first. Once players are sure it is a legal move, the line is darkened.

6. Players continue taking turns connecting letters until no more connections are possible. The player to make the last successful connection is the winner.

Game Board: Alphamazement, Mathamazement

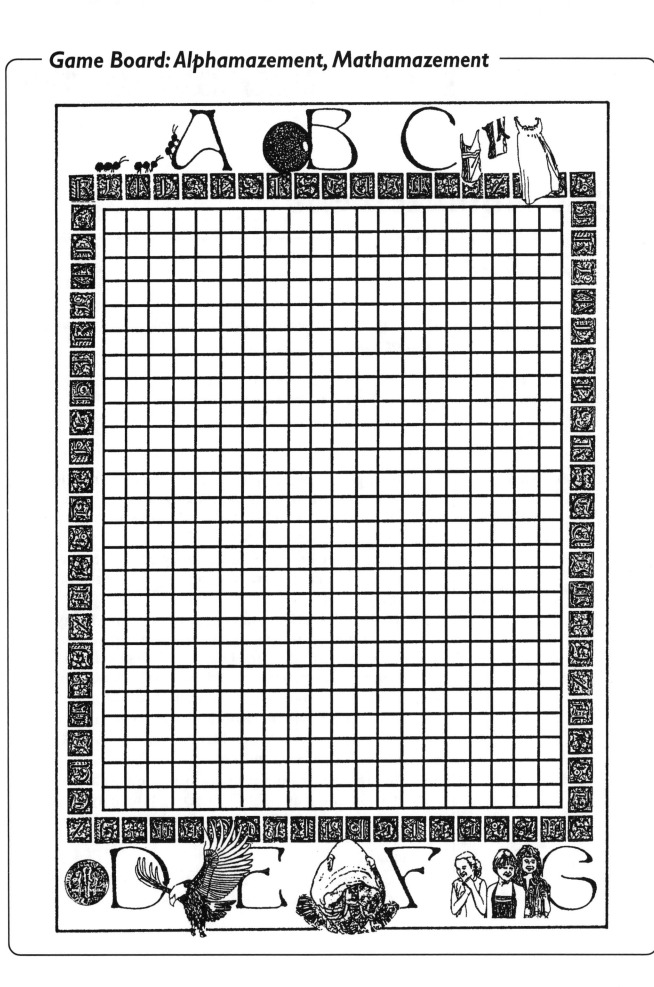

Mathamazement

Number of Players	2
Object	To be the last player to draw an unbroken line between a pair of numbers
Materials	copies of game board (page 77) pencils or pens

Playing the Game

1. Using pen or pencil, players take turns writing the numerals from *1* to *15* in the squares on the game board. The numbers should be scattered randomly around the board and spaced well apart.

2. Players then write the numerals from *1* to *15* a second time, once again scattering them randomly around the board.

3. The first player then draws a line that connects any pair of numbers on the board. The line must travel through the squares on the game board either vertically or horizontally. Zigzagging is permitted—the connecting line may have any number of right angle turns.

4. The second player then connects any other pair of numbers in the same manner. Players continue taking turns connecting pairs of numbers.

5. The connecting lines may not pass through any square that contains a number. Connecting lines may not cross other connecting lines. Once a line has passed through a square, no other line may be drawn through that same square.

6. Each line should be drawn lightly at first. Once players are sure it is a legal move, the line should be darkened.

Mathamazement (continued)

Playing the Game

7. Players continue taking turns connecting pairs of numbers until no more connections are possible. The player to make the last successful connection is the winner.

Variation

Players write the numerals from *1* to *50* randomly in the squares on the game board. They then take turns connecting any number with a factor or multiple of that number. Players score points equal to the sum of the two numbers they connect. Play follows all other rules described above.

Sprouts

John Horton Conway and Michael Stewart Paterson created this game.

Number of Players	2
Object	To be the last player to connect two dots with a line
Materials	paper pencils
Playing the Game	1. One player draws two to five dots on a sheet of paper. Beginners should start with two or three dots. 2. The second player draws a line starting at one dot and ending at any dot. A line may be drawn between two dots, or a line may start at a dot and return to that same dot. The line may be as straight or as curved as the player chooses. The player then places another dot somewhere on the line she drew. 3. The first player then takes a turn drawing a line beginning and ending at a dot, and placing an additional dot on that line. 4. No line may cross another line. 5. No dot may have more than three lines connected to it. 6. The last player who can connect two dots with a line is the winner.

Sprouts (continued)

Playing the Game

Sample Game

See figure 5, which illustrates the following game.

A. First player draws two dots.

B. Second player connects dots 1 and 2, and draws dot 3.

C. First player connects dots 1 and 2, and draws dot 4.

D. Second player connects dots 1 and 4, and draws dot 5. Dots 1 and 4 are now full.

E. First player connects dots 3 and 5, and draws dot 6. Dots 3 and 5 are now full.

F. Second player connects dots 2 and 6, and draws dot 7. Dots 2 and 5 are now full. No other moves are possible, so second player wins.

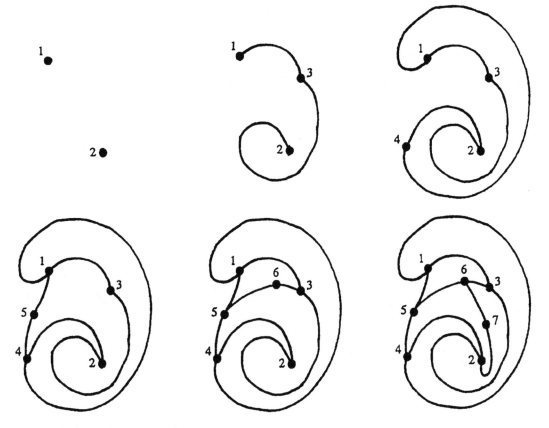

Figure 5. Sample game of Sprouts

Crosswalk

An active version of an old brainteaser

This puzzle requires teamwork and cooperation. It can be done! It can even be done more than once. Once players solve the puzzle, they should try it again to prove they understand how it works.

Number of Players

6

Object

To have all six players exchange positions on the playing field

Materials

7 carpet squares

square-foot sheets of cardboard or other similar flat objects to stand on, or playground chalk to mark squares on a side walk or blacktop

Playing the Game

1. Arrange the seven squares of carpet or cardboard on the ground in a straight line, leaving about 6 inches between squares (see figure 6). Three players stand on squares A, B, and C, facing center square D. Three other players stand on squares E, F, and G, also facing the center square.

Figure 6. Beginning Crosswalk

Crosswalk (continued)

Playing the Game

2. The players' task is to exchange positions so that each group of three players ends up standing in the squares previously occupied by the other three.

3. Players may move in one of two ways: a player may step forward one square onto an empty square, or a player may "jump" forward around one other player onto an empty square immediately beyond that player.

4. Players may not move backward. When the players reach an impasse, they must return to their original positions and begin again.

Source: *Silver Bullets,* by Karl Rohnke, Dubuque, Iowa, Kendall/Hunt Publishing, 1984. Used with permission.

Magic Square

An active version of an old brainteaser

Number of Players	8
Object	To have all eight players move to the correct positions on the playing field
Materials	8 large index cards numbered 1 through 8 in large print 9 carpet squares, foot-square sheets of cardboard, or other similar flat objects to stand on, or playground chalk to mark squares on a sidewalk or blacktop
Playing the Game	1. Arrange the 9 squares in a 3-by-3 grid on the ground. Each square should be numbered 1 through 9, in order. Shuffle the numbered index cards. Place one card face down on each square of the playing field except the center square. 2. Each player steps on one of the squares, leaving the center square unoccupied. Players pick up the cards; they then try to rearrange themselves so that they are standing on the corresponding numbered squares of the playing field. 3. Players may move only by stepping to the one square on the playing field that is currently vacant. Only one player may move at a time. Players may move only vertically or horizontally on the playing field; they may not step diagonally.
Variation	Fifteen players may play a more challenging version of this game on a 4-by-4 playing field. Leave any one of the four center squares without a card at the beginning of the game.

Maxey

Number of Players	2
Object	To score the most points by placing toothpicks
Materials	10 toothpicks paper pencil
Playing the Game	1. Draw seven vertical lines on the paper, with each pair being a little closer than the length of a toothpick.
	2. Players decide who will play first. After the first game, the loser of the previous game plays first. Each player gets five toothpicks.
	3. Players take turns placing toothpicks on the game board. A player may either place a toothpick on one of the vertical lines, or form a horizontal bridge between two adjacent toothpicks that are already on vertical lines. Only one bridge may be made between any two vertical toothpicks.
	4. Players score one point each time they place a toothpick on a vertical line next to another line that already holds a toothpick. Players score two points each time they form a bridge between two adjacent toothpicks.
	5. The player with the most points after all ten toothpicks have been placed is the winner.

Source: Gyles Brandreth, *World's Best Indoor Games*, New York, Pantheon Books, 1981. Used with permission.

Mancala

A traditional African game

Number of Players	2
Object	To clear your side of the board of all tokens
Materials	14 paper or plastic cups 36 beans, beads, or other tokens

Playing the Game

1. Arrange a set of 14 cups as shown in figure 7. An egg carton with a cup on each end may also be used. Traditionally, this game is played on a wooden or clay board with 14 pits. It is also played in pits dug into the ground.

O O O O O O

O   **O**

O O O O O O

Figure 7. Arrangement of Mancala cups

2. Place three tokens in each of the six cups on either side of the game board. No tokens are placed in the end cups.
3. Each player "owns" all the cups on his side of the game board. Neither player owns the end cups.
4. Players decide who will play first. After the first game, the loser of the previous game plays first. The first player takes all the tokens from any cup on his side of the board. He distributes them counterclockwise, placing one token in each cup, starting with the cup to the right of the cup he emptied. The end cups are included in this distribution.

Mancala (continued)

Playing the Game

5. In turn, players continue removing the tokens from one of their cups and distributing them counterclockwise.

6. When a player's last of one cup's tokens lands in an end cup, he gets another turn.

7. When the last token a player is distributing lands in an empty cup on the opponent's side of the board, the player picks up whatever tokens are in the cup opposite that one (on his own side of the board). He continues distributing those tokens as described in step 3.

8. The first player to empty all the cups on his side of the board is the winner.

Wari

A traditional African game, one of many Mancala variations

Number of Players	2
Object	To collect more tokens than your opponent
Materials	14 paper or plastic cups 48 beans, beads, or other tokens
Playing the Game	

1. Arrange a set of 14 cups as in Mancala (see figure 7, page 86). Traditionally, this game is played on a wooden or clay board with 14 pits. It may also be played in pits dug into the ground.

2. Each player "owns" the six cups or pits on her side. Each player also owns the end cup on her right, which is the scoring cup, or store. To start the game, players place four tokens in each cup on either side of the board. No tokens are placed in the stores.

3. Players decide who will play first. After the first game, the loser of the previous game plays first. The first player takes all the tokens from any cup on her side of the board. She distributes them counterclockwise, placing one token in each cup, starting with the cup to the right of the cup she emptied. The end cups are included in this distribution.

4. If the last of a cup's tokens lands in her own store, a player gets another turn.

5. If the last token a player is distributing lands in an empty cup on the opponent's side of the board, the player picks up whatever tokens are in the cup opposite that one (on her own side of the board). She continues distributing those tokens as described in step 3.

6. The game ends when all six cups on one side of the board are empty. The player with tokens remaining gathers them and adds them to her store.

7. Players then count the number of tokens in their stores. The player with the most tokens is the winner.

Congklak

Number of Players	2
Object	To finish with the most shells or beads in a store and other cups at the end of the game
Materials	12 small cups 50 beads, beans, shells, or other tokens
Playing the Game	1. Arrange a set of cups as shown in figure 8.

O O O O O

O   **O**

O O O O O

Figure 8. Arrangement of Congklak cups

2. Place five tokens in each of the five cups on either side of the game board. No tokens are placed in the end cups.
3. One player "owns" all the cups on one side of the game board. The other player owns all the cups on the other side. Each player owns the end cup, or "store," on his right.
4. Players decide who will play first. After the first game, the loser of the previous game plays first. The first player takes all the tokens from any cup on his side of the board. The player distributes the tokens clockwise, placing one token in each cup, starting with the cup to the left of the cup he emptied. The player's own store is included in this distribution, but the opponent's store is not.

Congklak (continued)

Playing the Game

5. When a player drops the last token he is distributing in a cup other than the store, he takes all the tokens from that cup and continues distributing them around the board.

6. If the last token in a player's hand drops into an empty cup on his side of the board, and if there are tokens in the opponent's cup directly opposite it, the player takes all the tokens from the opposite cup and places them in his store.

7. A player's turn is over when he drops the last token he is distributing into an empty cup on his side of the board and the opposing cup is empty, when the last token lands in an empty cup on the opponent's side, or when the last token lands in his own store. The other player then takes his turn.

8. The game is over when one player has no tokens left on his side of the board. The other player adds his remaining tokens to his store. Each player then counts all the tokens in his store. The player with the most tokens is the winner.

Tac-Tix

A game created by Danish mathematician and writer Piet Hein

Number of Players 2

Object To force your opponent to pick up the last toothpick

Materials 16 toothpicks or other small tokens

Playing the Game
1. Arrange the sixteen toothpicks in an array of four rows and four columns as shown in figure 9.

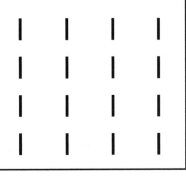

Figure 9. Arrangement of toothpicks for Tac-Tix

2. Players decide who will play first. After the first game, the loser of the previous game plays first.
3. The first player picks up one or more toothpicks from any row or any column of the array. If the player takes more than one, she may take only adjacent toothpicks.
4. The second player then takes one or more adjacent toothpicks from any row or any column.

Tac-Tix (continued)

5. Players continue alternating turns. Two or more toothpicks cannot be taken on a single turn if they are separated by a gap left by a previous move. For example, suppose a player had the following toothpicks remaining at his turn:

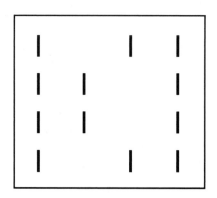

The player could not take all three toothpicks in any row, nor could she take both toothpicks in the third column.

6. The player who takes the last toothpick loses.

Source: Gyles Brandreth, *World's Best Indoor Games*, New York, Pantheon Books, 1981. Used with permission.

Nim

Number of Players	2
Object	To pick up the last playing piece on the board
Materials	12 tokens such as coins, beans, toothpicks
Playing the Game	1. Players place the 12 tokens in three rows: a row of 3, a row of 4, and a row of 5.
	2. Players decide who will play first. After the first game, the loser of the previous game plays first.
	3. In turn, each player picks up from one to all of the tokens on any one of the three rows.
	4. Players take turns picking up tokens until the last one is removed. The player who removes the last token loses.
Variations	1. Play the game as described above. The player who picks up the last token is the winner.
	2. Play the game as described above, except on each turn, a player may pick up no more than 3 tokens from the same row.
	3. Play the game as described above with 15 tokens in rows of 3, 5, and 7.

Supernim

Number of Players	2
Object	To score points by picking up the last playing piece in each section of the board
Materials	copy of game board (page 96) game tokens

Playing the Game

1. Players decide who will play first. After the first game, the loser of the previous game plays first.
2. Place one token in each space of the game board. Players take turns removing tokens from the board, following the rules of Nim. In turn, players pick up from one to all of the tokens on any one of the three rows in any section.
3. A player scores 1 point each time he takes the last token in each of the six sections of the board. The player to take the last token in the last remaining section scores two points. The player to score the most points is the winner.

Variations

1. Play the game as described above, except on each turn, a player may pick up no more than 3 tokens from the same row.
2. Arrange the game board and play as described above. A player scores 1 point each time *the opponent* takes the last token in any one of the six sections of the board. The player scores 2 points when *the opponent* removes the last token on the entire board. The player to score the most points is the winner.

Supernim (continued)

3. The first player places tokens in each of the six sections of the game board. Each section must have at least one token in it. It may have no more than the twelve allowed for. At least one section must have two or more tokens. At least one row must have two or more tokens. Beginning with the second player, players take turns removing tokens from the board, following the rules of Nim. The player to remove the last token is the winner.

4. Play the game described in variation 3. The player who picks up the last token is the loser.

Game Board: Supernim

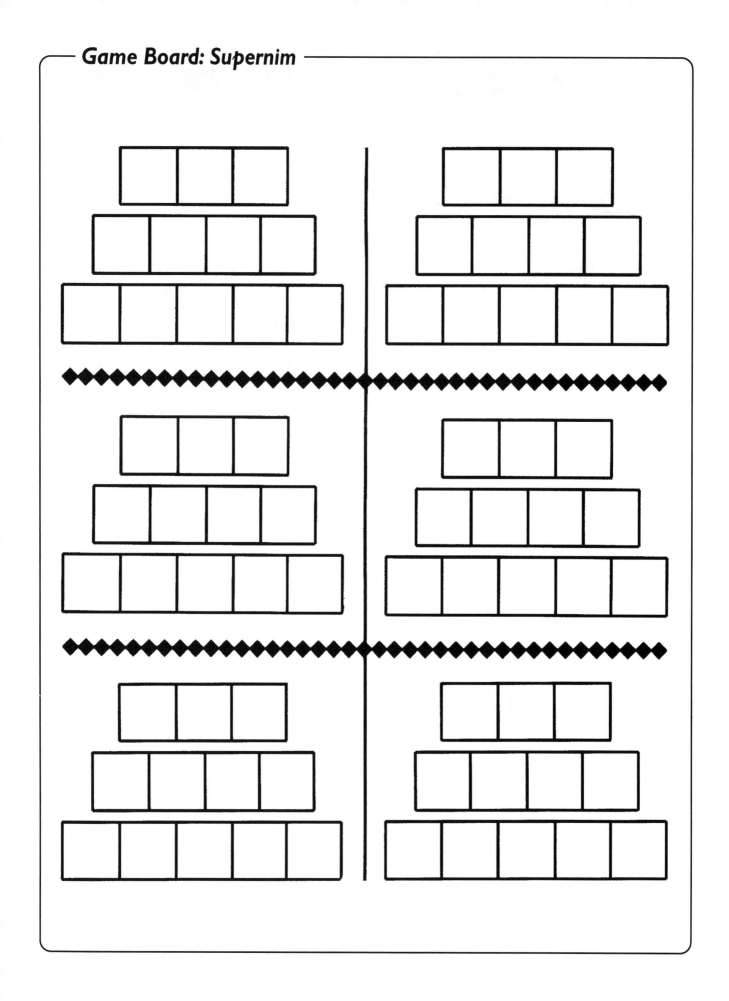

Five Dice

Number of Players	any number
Object	To use various mathematical operations to reach a target number
Materials	5 dice 1-minute timer paper pencil
Playing the Game	

1. One player is chosen to be the timekeeper. The first player rolls one of the dice. The number that turns up becomes the target number.

2. The first player then rolls the other four dice. The timekeeper starts the timer. Players have one minute (or some other agreed-upon amount of time) to use all four working numbers on those dice to calculate the target number in some way. Calculations must be written on paper.

   For example suppose the target number is 5, and the other four dice are 1, 4, 3, and 3. One player might reach the target number by adding 1 and 4 to get 5, multiplying by 3 to get 15, and then dividing by 3. Another player might multiply 4 times 3 to get 12, then divide by 3 to get 4, and add 1.

3. Each player who calculates a way to reach the target number earns a number of points equal to the target number. If players can reach the target number in more than one way, they earn an extra point for each additional calculation.

Five Dice (continued)

Playing the Game

4. Dice are then passed to the next player, who rolls a new target number and a new set of working numbers. The player with the highest number of points at the end of the game is the winner.

Variations

1. For higher target numbers, players may roll two dice and add or multiply them.
2. For a more competitive version of the game, have the first person who correctly calculates the target number score a bonus point.

2001

Number of Players	2 or more
Object	To be the first player to reach 2001 (or some other agreed-upon number)
Materials	a pair of dice paper for each player pencil for each player
Playing the Game	1. Players sit in a circle. Players roll a die to decide who will play first. After the first game, the loser of the previous game plays first. The first player sets the target number—either 2001 or some other number of that player's choice. The first player then rolls the dice, and all players write the sum of the numbers on the two dice on their papers. 2. The second player then rolls the dice. The players write that sum on their papers. Each player then performs any mathematical operation—addition, subtraction, multiplication, or division—on the two numbers. This and all other calculations must result in whole numbers. 3. The third player rolls the dice. The players write that number on their papers and perform a mathematical operation with it and the result of the previous operation. 4. Play continues around the circle until one (or more) players' calculations result in the target number. The players who achieve that result win. 5. Players compete in an agreed-upon number of rounds. The player who wins the most rounds is the overall winner of the game.
Variation	As each player rolls the dice in turn, only that player uses the resulting number. All other rules remain the same.

One to Twelve

Number of Players	2
Object	To get the highest score by rolling a pair of dice
Materials	pair of dice 12 index cards numbered 1 through 12
Playing the Game	1. Place the 12 numbered index cards face up on the table. Players decide who will play first. After the first game, the loser of the previous game plays first.
	2. The first player rolls the dice. She may choose to take a card marked with the value of either die, or the card with the value of the sum of the dice. Once a card has been chosen, it is out of play and may not be used again for the remainder of the round.
	3. The second player then rolls. She too takes a card that represents either the value of one of the dice or their sum—as long as that number has not already been taken.
	4. Players continue taking turns, rolling dice and choosing cards, until all the cards have been taken. If no cards may be taken on a particular roll of the dice, the player simply passes the dice to her opponent.
	5. Each player adds the total of all the cards she has claimed. The player with the highest total is the winner.
Variation	A similar game may be played with 3 dice and 18 cards. Players may then select the result from any one die, or any combination of two or three dice on each turn.

MADS

Multiply, Add, Divide, Subtract

Number of Players	2 to 5
Object	To use various calculations to reach a target number
Materials	1 or 2 decks of playing cards paper pencil
Playing the Game	1. Remove all the face cards from one or two decks of playing cards. Players sit in a circle. One player shuffles the cards and deals four cards face down to each player. 2. The dealer turns up the next card in the deck and places it in the center of the table. The number on that card becomes the target number. 3. Using the basic operations, players attempt to use all four numbers on their cards to calculate the target number in some way. Suppose the target number is 8 and a player's cards are 9, 4, 3, and an ace. The player might reach the target number by adding 1 and 3 to get 4, dividing 4 by 4 to get 1, and then subtracting 1 from 9 to reach the target. 4. The first player to figure out a way to reach the target number with all four of his cards places them face up on the table and says "MADS!" All other players must immediately place their cards face down on the table. The player then shows everyone the calculation with the cards. If the calculation is correct, the round is over. The player puts the four cards aside in his scoring pile. The dealer gives the winning player four new cards and turns up a new target card for the next round of play.

MADS (continued)

Playing the Game

5. If the player's calculation is incorrect, the player must give one card from his hand to each of the other players to be placed in their scoring pile. At the dealer's signal, the remaining players continue trying to reach the target number. The player who was incorrect may not participate for the remainder of the round. At the end of the round, the dealer replenishes that player's hand from the deck.

6. In case of a tie—if two players call "MADS!" simultaneously—both players must explain their calculations. If both are correct, each player gets to put two cards in his scoring piles, and the dealer gives each player two new cards. If only one is correct, that player puts all four cards in his scoring pile, and the other player must distribute a card to each player. If neither player is correct, each of them must give a card to the other players. The dealer replaces cards as needed at the end of the round.

7. If no one can reach the target number with the cards in their hands, the dealer places the target card at the bottom of the deck and turns over a new target number.

8. Play continues until there are no longer enough cards to play another round. Players then count the number of cards in their scoring piles. The player with the most cards is the winner.

Variations

1. Leave the four jacks in the deck. These are wild cards, and may be used to represent any number from 1 to 10. If the dealer turns up a jack as a target number, he simply places it at the bottom of the deck and turns over a new card.

2. Players may play with a full deck, assigning the following values:

   Jack = 11

   Queen = 12

   King = 13

Top Dog

Number of Players	2 to 4
Object	To reach the highest possible total
Materials	4 dice paper for each player pencil for each player electronic calculators (optional)

Playing the Game

1. Players roll a die to choose who will play first. After the first game, the loser of the previous game plays first. The first player then rolls all four dice. She may then either multiply all four numbers together, or write the numbers as two, two-digit numbers and add them. Suppose the player rolls 3, 3, 5, and 2. She may multiply them together (2 x 3 x 3 x 5) and use the product (90), or she may write them as 52 and 33, then add them to get 85.

2. Each player tries to get the highest possible number on each turn. In the example above, the player should take the option of multiplying, since that produces the higher value.

3. Players take turns rolling the four dice, then adding or multiplying the resulting numbers.

4. Play continues for an agreed-upon number of rounds (usually ten or fewer). Each player adds the result of each new round to the total of previous rounds. The player with the highest total at the end of the game is the winner.

Huvnuts

Number of Players	2 to 6
Object	To be the first to reach 5000
Materials	5 dice paper pencil
Playing the Game	

1. Players decide who will play first. After the first game, the loser of the previous game plays first. Play continues clockwise around the table.

2. In turn, each player rolls all five dice, scoring in the following manner:

   A 1 scores 100 points

   A 5 scores 50 points

   Three of a kind scores 100 times the face value of the number rolled (three 4s count 400 points)

   Three 1s score 1000 points

3. A player must score 550 or higher on one roll before he is allowed to enter the game and begin accumulating points. In other words, at the beginning of the game, any scores below 550 are not recorded.

4. After a player has entered the game with a 550 or higher, a player must score at least 50 points on each roll in order to proceed. If the player scores zero, he passes the dice to the player to his left.

5. A player who has rolled at least 50 points may choose to take the points he has scored, or to continue rolling the dice in an attempt to accumulate more points. A player must put aside at least one scoring die if he chooses to roll for more points. For example, suppose a player rolls

Huvnuts (continued)

Playing the Game

a 1, two 3s, a 5, and a 6. The player may either (a) add 150 points (the 1 and the 5) to his total score and pass the dice; (b) put aside the 1 and roll the remaining four dice to try for more points; or (c) put aside the 1 and the 5 and roll the remaining three dice to try for more points.

6. In either b or c, the dice that have been put aside may not be included as part of a three of a kind when the player rolls again.

7. If a player chooses to roll again and scores a zero, he forfeits all the points he has accumulated during the turn and must pass the dice.

8. When a player rolls scoring numbers on all five dice, either with the first roll or on later rolls after setting dice aside as in rule 5, he must roll all five dice again. If that roll does not score points, the player scores a zero and must pass the dice. However, if the next roll scores any points, the player may take the accumulated points or keep playing. For example, suppose our player chose option b in step 5. On the next roll, he rolled three 4s and a 1. He would have a total score of 600, but would be required to roll the dice again. If he scored at least 50 points on that next roll, he could add that to the 600 and stop, or continue trying for even more points.

9. The first player to reach a score of exactly 5000 is the winner. Scoring beyond 5000 is not permitted. A player with a score of 4,750 would have to pass the dice if he rolled three sixes, for example, and try to hit 5000 on the next turn.

Variation

Huvnuts is a gambling game. Playing with chips, beans, or other counters may add extra interest. Each player antes a chip at the beginning of the game. Players must add another chip to the pot each time they score a zero. The first player to 5000 wins the entire pot.

Factor Stix

Number of Players	2 to 8
Object	To be the first player to reach 100 points (or some other agreed-upon score)
Materials	1 or 2 sets of plastic pick-up sticks paper for each player pencil for each player
Playing the Game	1. Players sit in a circle around a table or on the floor. Players decide who will play first. After the first game, the loser of the previous game plays first.
	2. The first player picks up the bundle of pick-up sticks in one hand. With one end of the bundle touching the playing surface, the player lets the sticks fall and scatter.
	3. The first player then begins picking up sticks, one at a time. Each stick must be picked up without moving any other sticks. If another stick is moved, the player's turn is over.
	4. Yellow sticks are worth 1 point, green sticks are worth 2 points, blue sticks are worth 3 points, and red sticks are worth 5 points. When a player successfully picks up a stick, he adds the value of that stick to his total score. After the first stick, players may pick up only a stick with a numerical value that is a factor of their current total score.
	5. The player continues picking up sticks one by one. She plays until she moves another stick, or until no stick that is a factor of the player's total may be picked up. Play then passes to the player to her left.

Factor Stix (continued)

Playing the Game

6. The black stick may have any value between 1 and 11. If the black stick may be picked up on a player's turn, she decides what value it will have and announces it to the other players. Its value must be a factor of the player's total score. After a player retrieves the black stick, she may use it as a tool to help lift and pick up other sticks. If a player fails to pick up the black stick, other players are free to assign a different value to it in their turns.

7. If play passes completely around the group without any-one scoring, everyone must subtract 1 point from her score. The player whose turn it is collects all the sticks and scatters them again. Play resumes.

8. The first player to reach a score of 100, or some other agreed-upon total, is the winner.

Taxman

A paper and pencil version of an old computer game

Number of Players	2
Object	To score the highest number of points
Materials	paper pencil
Playing the Game	1. One player (the taxman) writes a master list of all the integers from *1* to *20* (or to some top number less than 100) on a piece of paper. The other player (the taxpayer) will play first.
	2. The taxpayer selects any number from the list. He crosses that number out on the game sheet and writes it on his own score sheet.
	3. The taxman then gets all the factors of that number on his list. The taxman crosses the factors off the list and writes them on his score sheet.
	4. The taxman must score on each move, so the taxpayer may not take a number that has no factors remaining on the list.
	5. Play continues in this manner until no numbers with factors remain on the master list. When no number with factors is left, the taxman gets all the remaining numbers.
	6. Each player adds all the numbers he has taken. The player with the highest total wins the round.
	7. Players then reverse roles. The first player to win two rounds in a row—one as the taxman and one as the taxpayer—wins the match.

Buzz

Number of Players	3 or more
Object	To avoid saying certain numbers while counting
Materials	none

Playing the Game

1. Players sit in a circle. The first player chooses any number from 3 to 9. Players begin to count, with each saying the next number in turn. However, they must say *buzz* instead of the chosen number, multiples of that number, or numbers that contain it as a digit. For example, suppose the number chosen is 7. Players would then say, "One, two, three, four, five, six, *buzz*, eight, nine, ten, eleven, twelve, thirteen, *buzz*, fifteen, sixteen, *buzz*, eighteen, nineteen, twenty, *buzz*, twenty-two," and so on.

2. Players count around the circle until someone makes a mistake. That player is then out. Counting continues until all players but one have been eliminated. The last remaining player is the winner and gets to choose the number to avoid for the next round.

Variation

Fizz-Buzz: Players choose two numbers to avoid. One must be replaced by *fizz* and the other by *buzz*. If a number contains both numbers, or is a multiple of both numbers, players must say *fizz-buzz*. For example, if the two selected numbers were 3 and 5, the count would be, "One, two, *buzz*, four, *fizz*, *buzz*, seven, eight, *buzz*, *fizz*, eleven, *buzz*, *buzz*, fourteen, *fizz-buzz*, sixteen," and so on.

Prime Dominoes

Number of Players	2 to 6
Object	To collect the most dominos by the end of the game
Materials	set of dominos (double sixes, double nines, or double twelves for experts) electronic calculators (optional)
Playing the Game	1. Players sit in a circle. All dominos are placed face down in the center of the table. One player (the dealer) shuffles the dominos. Each player selects five dominos from the pile. 2. The dealer then selects one domino at random from the pile and turns it face up. 3. The player to the left of the dealer plays first. She adds the total number of dots on the upturned domino to the total number of dots on any one domino in her hand in an attempt to reach a sum that is a prime number. 4. If the player may make a prime number, she places the domino from her hand face up on the table next to the upturned domino. The player announces the prime number and then collects both dominos for her scoring pile. The player then draws a domino from the pile to replace the one from her hand and overturns a new domino for the next player to use. 5. If the player cannot make a prime number, she must discard any one of the dominos in her hand, face up. The player then replaces that domino by drawing another from the pile. The next player may use either or both of the upturned dominos to make a prime number.

Prime Dominoes (continued)

Playing the Game

6. Play continues in this manner until all the dominos in the pile have been turned over and used. At the end of the game, when no more dominos are left to draw, a player must simply pass if she cannot make a prime. The game ends when the last upturned domino is taken or when no one can make a play. The player who has collected the most dominos in her scoring pile is the winner.

Variation

This game may be played with players having to reach any multiple of a particular number (five, let's say, or seven), or a square.

Twenty Questions

Still one of the best deductive logic games around!

Number of Players	any number
Object	To identify the game leader's secret object within twenty guesses
Materials	none
Playing the Game	1. Choose one player to be the game leader. The leader secretly chooses an object in the room, being careful not to give it away by looking at it directly.
	2. The rest of the players begin asking questions about the secret object. They may ask only questions that can be answered with a *yes* or *no*. For example, "Is it red?" is an acceptable question. "What color is it?" is not. The leader calls on players to guess and keeps track of the number of questions asked.
	3. Players are allowed only twenty questions in which to identify the object. Players must listen carefully to each question and its answer to avoid repetition. They should try to eliminate large categories of objects before guessing specific objects.
	4. If the players ask twenty questions without identifying the secret object, the leader tells them what the object is. The leader then chooses another player to lead the next round of the game. If one of the players identifies the secret object, that player becomes the game leader for the next round of play.

Twenty Questions *(continued)*

Variations

1. Critters: The leader chooses any animal in the world.

2. Animal, Vegetable, or Mineral: The leader chooses any object in the world. He then tells the players whether it is an animal, vegetable, or mineral. For example, paper is vegetable because it is made of wood; a soda can is mineral; a leather belt is animal.

3. Careers: The leader chooses an occupation.

4. Celebrities: The leader chooses a famous person, living or dead.

5. Mystery Number: The leader chooses a number between 0 and some upper limit, perhaps 1,000 or 1,000,000.

Mystery Box

A cooperative version of Twenty Questions

Number of Players	Any number
Object	For all players to work together, asking questions, until everyone knows what is in the mystery box
Materials	a small empty box such as a shoe box
Playing the Game	

1. Choose one player to be the game leader. The leader holds a small, closed box. Using his imagination, the leader "puts" an object into the box. The object need not be small enough to actually fit in the box.

2. Players ask yes-or-no questions in an effort to identify the object in the box, as in Twenty Questions. However, players may not guess specific objects. They may only ask descriptive questions about it. For example, "Is it sharp?" is an acceptable question; "Is it a knife?" is not.

3. If a player asks "Is it a _____" the leader must answer "I don't know" whether the guess is correct or not.

4. The goal is for everyone to identify the object in the box without anyone ever naming it. When players think they know the object, they should ask further questions that will help other players figure it out. For example, if a player thinks a pencil is in the box, he might ask the question, "Does it have lead in it?" "Is it usually yellow?" or "Does it have a rubber eraser on the end?" The player must not ask "Is it a pencil?"

5. When the game leader thinks everyone knows what is in the box, he asks the group if there is anyone who doesn't know. If someone says he's not sure, the questioning continues.

6. The game is over when everyone knows what is in the box. The game leader may ask someone to name the object, or he may choose to leave it unnamed, since everyone already knows what it is anyway. The leader then chooses someone else to lead the next round of the game.

Going to Chicago

Number of Players	Any number
Object	To join the game leader on the "trip" by figuring out the category of objects she is taking with her
Materials	none
Playing the Game	

1. Players choose someone to serve as the game leader. The leader thinks of a category of things to take with her on her imaginary trip. She then says, "I'm going to Chicago, and I'm taking a _____." She completes the sentence with an object that fits into the category.

2. The category the leader chooses may be as simple as "things that begin with the letter *S*." As players become more familiar with the game, the categories should become trickier—things with legs, things made of cloth, things that use electricity, and so on.

3. After the leader has told the players what she is taking to Chicago, they begin asking, "If I bring a _____ , may I go with you?" If the player names an object that fits the leader's category, the leader tells the player that she may join the trip. If the player names an object that doesn't fit the category, the leader says "No, but you may go if you bring a _____ ," naming an object that does fit the category.

4. The game continues until all players have correctly guessed a different object that fits the leader's category. The leader then chooses another player to lead the next round of the game.

My Fussy Neighbor

Number of Players	6 or more
Object	To figure out the leader's secret rule
Materials	none

Playing the Game

1. One player is chosen to be the game leader. He secretly chooses a category of words or objects that his neighbor "hates." For example, he may choose words that contain the letter *c*.

2. The leader then provides the rest of the players a single example of his category by stating, "My neighbor is very fussy. He loves _____ but he hates _____ ." For the example given in 1, he might say, "My neighbor is very fussy. He loves dogs but he hates cats."

3. The rest of the players try to determine the secret category by asking the leader questions. If the players' questions do not fit the category, the leader must answer by giving another example of the category. For example, one player might ask, "Does he hate birds?" The leader could say, "No, he likes birds but he hates crows."

4. When a player guesses correctly, the leader says, "Oh, you know my neighbor, too." That player now takes the place of the leader in responding to further questions from the other players. The player does not reveal the category. If the new leader answers another player's question incorrectly, the original game leader instructs him to rejoin the rest of the group and continue asking questions.

My Fussy Neighbor (continued)

Playing the Game

5. Players continue asking questions and taking turns in the leader's role when they are correct. The game continues until all the players have figured out the secret category.

6. Once players understand how the game is played, they may make it more difficult by choosing very challenging categories. For example, the leader might choose things made of wood, words of one syllable, objects of a certain color, or things found in a kitchen. The possibilities are endless.

Human Shuffle

Number of Players	10 or more
Object	To figure out what characteristic the game leader has used to divide players into groups
Materials	none
Playing the Game	1. Choose one person to act as game leader. The remaining players stand and wait for that player's instructions.

2. The game leader separates the players into two or more groups based on some characteristic that everyone in the subgroups have in common. The leader directs each player to stand with others that share that characteristic. The leader must not reveal the quality she is using to do the sorting.

3. Game leaders should start with easily visible characteristics such as hair color, type of shoes, or glasses. As players become more skilled, the leader may make categories more difficult to determine, such as whether or not players have pierced ears. The leader may even use qualities that are not visible at all, such as age or whether or not a player has brothers or sisters.

4. Leaders must be careful to choose categories that don't overlap. For example, the leader could divide players into groups of those wearing athletic shoes and those wearing sandals. It would not be acceptable to divide the players into those wearing shoes and people with black hair because those two categories may overlap.

5. After the leader divides the players into groups, the players must look at the grouping and try to figure out the characteristic the leader used to group them.

Human Shuffle (continued)

Playing the Game

6. The leader calls on players to guess how the groups have been created. The first player to guess correctly becomes the new game leader. The new leader redivides the players using new categories.

7. A player may identify a set of categories that the leader had not thought of, but which also would divide the group in the same way. In that case, the leader must indicate that the player is correct. However, players continue guessing until they identify the leader's method of dividing the group.

Witch Hunt

Number of Players	2
Object	To find an opponent's witch before he finds yours
Materials	copies of game board (page 121) pencil or pen

Playing the Game

1. Each player gets a copy of the game board. Players secretly position a witch by drawing a small, triangular witch's hat at one of the intersections on their boards. Players must be careful not to show each other their game boards.

2. Players decide who will play first. After the first game, the loser of the previous game plays first.

3. The first player guesses a location on the opponent's game board by calling out its coordinates. The player must call the X-coordinate (location across) first, followed by the Y-coordinate (location up or down). The player records his guess in the space provided at the bottom of the game board.

4. The second player repeats the guess aloud to verify it. Then he records the guess on his game board with a small dot placed on the appropriate coordinate. The second player then tells the first in which direction he needs to go to find the hidden witch. Players should use the cardinal directions (north, south, east, west) only if the witch is located exactly in one of those directions. Otherwise, they should tell the opponent to go northeast, northwest, southeast, or southwest.

5. The first player then records the direction of travel at the bottom of the game board, next to the coordinates he just guessed.

6. The second player now takes a turn guessing the location of the first player's witch. The first player marks the guess and tells which direction the second player needs to travel.

7. Players continue taking turns until one player finds the exact location of the opponent's witch.

Game Board: Witch Hunt

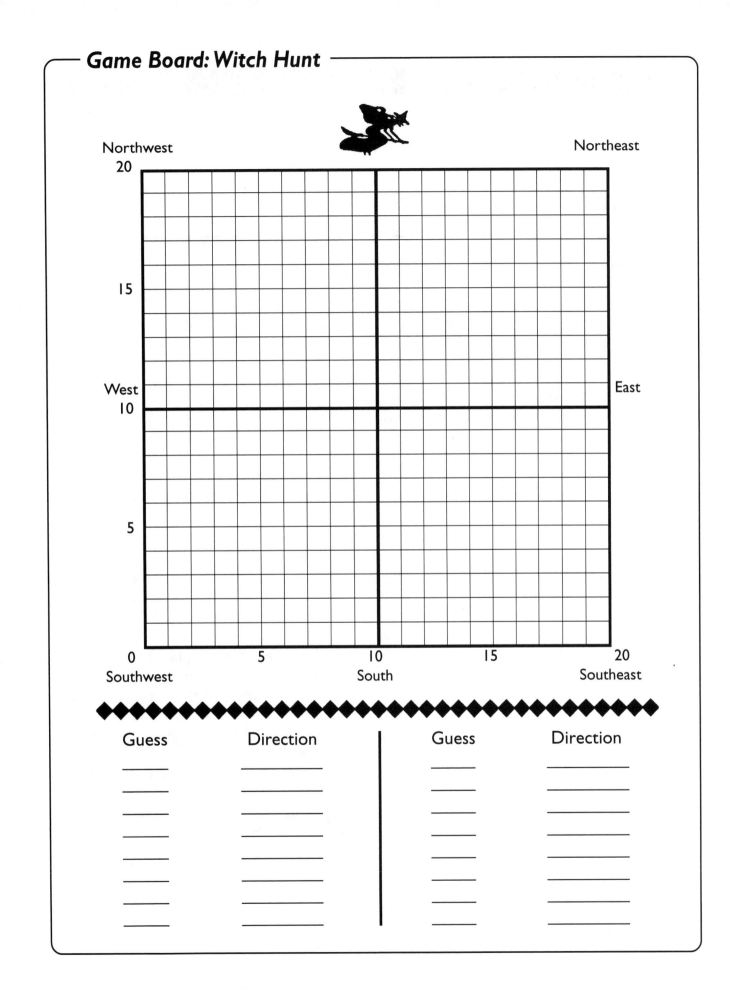

Northwest   Northeast

20

15

West
10

5

0   5   10   15   20
Southwest   South   Southeast

East

Guess	Direction		Guess	Direction
_____	_____		_____	_____
_____	_____		_____	_____
_____	_____		_____	_____
_____	_____		_____	_____
_____	_____		_____	_____
_____	_____		_____	_____
_____	_____		_____	_____

Salvo

Number of Players	2
Object	To sink all your opponent's ships before she sinks yours
Materials	copies of game board (page 124) pencils or pens

Playing the Game

1. Each player gets a copy of the game board. Once the game begins, players must make sure they don't see each other's game board.

2. If players prefer, they may use larger or smaller grids drawn on graph paper instead of the game board provided. Players may also agree to use a different assortment of ships than those given. Each player must use the same size grid and the same number and kinds of ships as her opponent.

3. In the grid labeled "My Fleet," each player draws the outlines of her ships. Each player should have one aircraft carrier (6 squares), one battleship (5 squares), one cruiser (4 squares), two destroyers (3 squares each), and two submarines (2 squares each) on the grid. Ships may be placed anywhere on the grid. They must be drawn either vertically or horizontally. Ships may not overlap one another.

4. After players have placed their ships on their grids, play may begin. Players decide who fires first. After the first game, the loser of the previous game fires first.

Salvo (continued)

Playing the Game

5. The first player fires a "salvo" of five shots. A shot is fired by calling out the letter and number of a square in the enemy fleet grid (D7 or F3, for example). The player who is firing marks each shot in the Enemy Fleet grid, using the number of the salvo. For example, marking each shot in the first salvo with a *1*, each shot in the second round with a *2*, and so on.)

6. After each shot, the opponent marks that square with an *X* in her fleet on the game board. The opponent should repeat the letter and number of each shot to the first player to make sure she has heard the information correctly.

7. After the first player has called all five shots, her opponent tells her which ships, if any, have been hit and with how many shots. Her opponent does not tell which shots made the hits. For example, she may say, "You got one hit in the cruiser," "No hits," or "Two in the battleship and one in a submarine," but not "G2 hit my aircraft carrier." If one of the ships has been sunk—completely filled in with shots—she must tell the player at the end of the salvo ("You sank my destroyer," for example.)

   The first player records this information by marking the salvo number in the appropriate number of squares of the ship outlines beneath the enemy fleet grid on the game board to help her locate and sink ships in later rounds.

8. The second player takes a turn firing a salvo of five shots. Players alternate turns until all of one player's ships have been sunk.

9. Each player gets five shots per salvo until her aircraft carrier has been sunk. After that, the player gets only three shots per salvo for the remainder of the game.

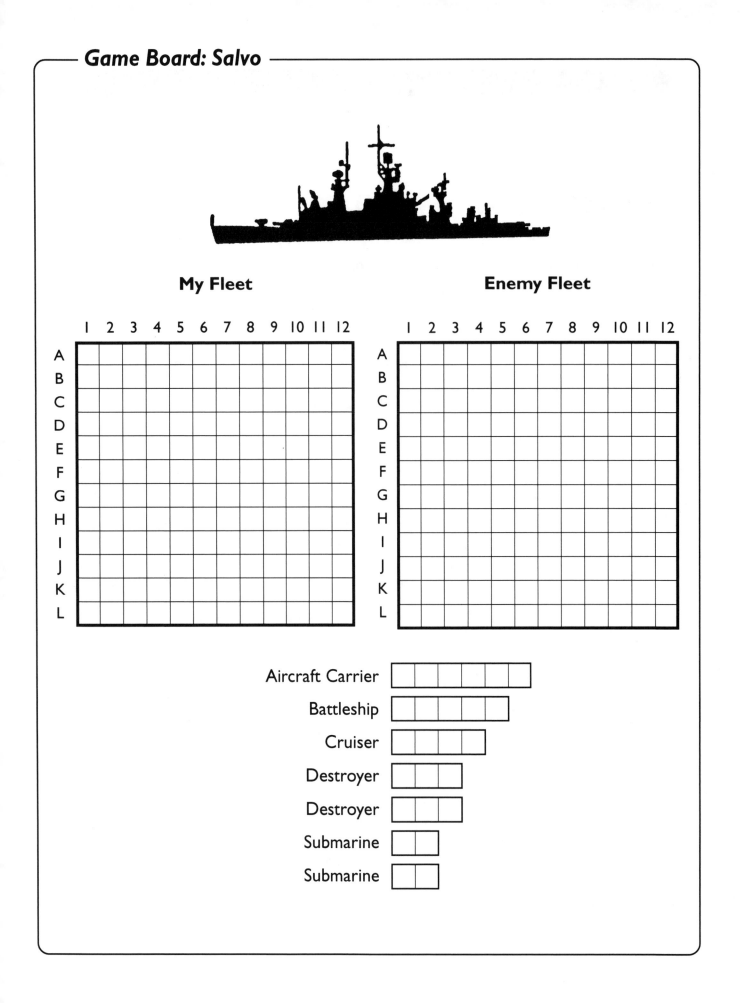

Game Board: Salvo

My Fleet

Enemy Fleet

Aircraft Carrier

Battleship

Cruiser

Destroyer

Destroyer

Submarine

Submarine

Astroclash

Number of Players	2
Object	To destroy your opponent's star fleet before he destroys yours
Materials	copies of game board (page 128) pencils or pens

Playing the Game

1. Each player gets a copy of the game board. Once play begins, players must make sure they don't see each other's game board.

2. In the grid labeled "My Fleet," each player draws the outlines of his ships, black holes, and force fields. Each player should have one planetoid (9 squares), one star cruiser (8 squares), two frigates (4 squares), three star fighters (3 squares), two force fields and two black holes (1 square each) on the grid. Ships, black holes, and force fields may be placed anywhere on the grid. They must be drawn either vertically or horizontally; ships may not overlap one another.

3. When both players have placed their ships on their grids, play may begin. Players decide who fires first. After the first game the loser of the previous game fires first.

4. The first player fires a salvo of five shots. A shot is fired by calling out the letter and number of a square in the Enemy Fleet grid (D7 or F3, for example). The first shot of each salvo is an atomic disintegrator. If it hits a ship, the entire ship is destroyed. The remaining 4 shots in a salvo are laser cannons that destroy only the single square they hit.

5. The player who is firing marks each shot in the Enemy Fleet grid, using the number of the salvo. (For example, marking each shot in the first salvo with a *1*, each shot in the second round with a *2*, and so on.) Atomic disintegrator shots are marked with a circle around the number.

Astroclash (continued)

Playing the Game

6. After a player fires a shot, the opponent marks that square with an X in the "My Fleet" section of the game board. The opponent should repeat the letter and number of each shot to the first player to make sure he heard the information correctly.

7. A shot that hits a black hole or force field must be reported immediately, before any more shots are fired. Otherwise, the player being fired upon waits until all five shots have been fired before reporting the results.

8. When a shot hits a black hole, the firing player loses the remainder of his turn because black holes absorb energy. The player being fired upon reports the results of the salvo (see rule 10), then begins his own salvo.

9. When a shot hits a force field, that shot is reflected back to the same square of the firing player's "My Fleet" grid. The firing player must immediately tell what, if anything, that reflected shot has hit. If an atomic disintegrator shot hits a force field and is reflected back to one of the firing player's ships, that entire ship is destroyed. Hitting a force field automatically ends a player's salvo. The player whose force field was hit reports the results of the rest of the salvo (see rule 10), then begins his turn to fire.

10. After the first player has called all five shots, the opponent tells him which ships, if any, have been hit, and with how many shots. The opponent does not tell which of the shots made the hits. For example, he might say something like "You got one hit in a frigate," "Two in the star cruiser and one in a straighter," or "No hits," but not "G2 hit my planetoid.") If one of the ships has been destroyed—completely filled in with shots—he must tell the player at the end of the salvo. ("You destroyed my star cruiser," for example.)

Astroclash (continued)

Playing the Game

11. The first player records this information by marking the salvo number in the appropriate number of squares of the ship outlines beneath the "Enemy Fleet" grid. This will help him locate and destroy the ships in later rounds.

12. If the atomic disintegrator has scored a hit, the opponent must report the location of all the squares in the ship that was destroyed. Both players then cross those squares out on their grids.

13. The second player now takes his turn firing a salvo of five shots. Players alternate turns until all of one player's ships have been sunk. A ship is not considered destroyed until all squares of the ship have been hit.

14. Each player gets one atomic disintegrator shot and four laser cannon shots per salvo until his planetoid has been destroyed. After that, the player gets only four laser cannon shots per salvo for the remainder of the game.

Game Board: Astroclash

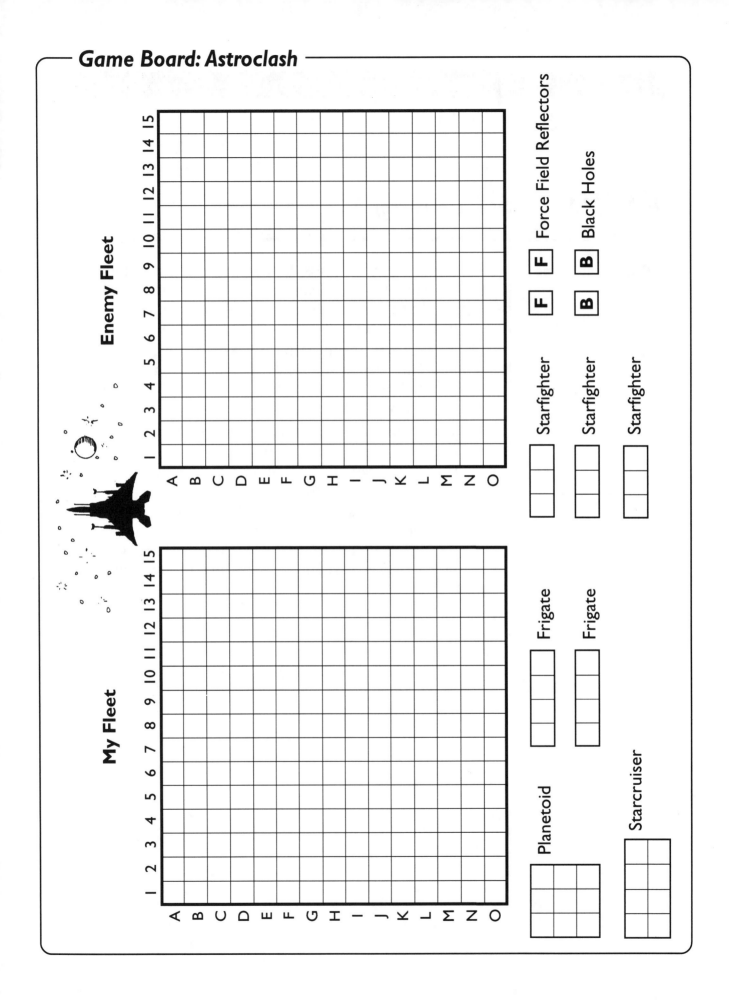

Enemy Fleet

My Fleet

Starfighter

Starfighter

Starfighter

F | **F** Force Field Reflectors

B | **B** Black Holes

Frigate

Frigate

Planetoid

Starcruiser

Bagels

A paper and pencil version of a classic computer game

Number of Players	2
Object	To figure out your opponent's secret number before she figures out yours
Materials	paper for each player pencil for each player

Playing the Game

1. Players fold a sheet of paper down the middle. Each player writes a secret 3-digit number on the right side of the paper. Players may use any 3 digits from *0* to *9*. No digit may be used more than once.

2. Players decide who will play first. After the first game, the loser of the previous game plays first.

3. The first player guesses any 3-digit number and writes down her guess on the left side of the paper. The second player writes the guess on the right side of her paper beneath the secret number. The player then responds to the guess by saying "fermi" for each digit the player has guessed correctly, in the correct location. She says "pico" for each digit the player has guessed correctly, but in the wrong location. She says "bagels" if none of the digits is correct.

4. The first player writes the opponent's response beside her guess. For example, suppose the second player's secret number is 508. If the first player's guess is 123, the second player says "bagels." If the first player's guess is 024, the second player says "pico" because there is a 0 in the secret number, but it is not in the first position. If the first player's guess is 890, the second player says "pico, pico" because there are an 8 and a 9 in the secret number, but not in the first and second place, respectively. If the first player's guess is 701, the second player says

Bagels (continued)

Number of Players

"fermi" because the 0 is in the secret number and in the second place. If the first player's guess is 802, the second player says "fermi, pico" because the 0 is in the secret number and in the same place as in the guess, and there is an 8 in the secret number but not in the first place. If the first player's guess is 805, the second player says "fermi, pico, pico."

5. Players take turns guessing each other's numbers and writing down their opponent's responses. The first player to figure out and guess her opponent's number correctly in her turn is the winner.

Crash

Number of Players	2
Object	To figure out the opponent's target word
Materials	paper for each player pencil for each player
Playing the Game	

1. Players decide on the number of letters to be used in the target words. Beginning players should start with 3- or 4-letter words. Players also decide who will play first. After the first game, the loser of the previous game plays first.

2. Each player draws a line down the center of the page, dividing the paper into two vertical columns. Each player then writes a secret target word at the top of the right column. Players should fold a flap of paper over their individual target words to make sure the opponents don't see them by accident.

3. Players take turns trying to guess their opponent's target word with test words. The guessing player writes his guess in the left column. The opposing player writes the guess beneath his target word in the right column. Test words must have the same number of letters as the target words. Target words and all test words must be real English words or words in the language in which players are playing.

4. A "crash" is a letter that appears in the same location in both the test word and the target word. Each time a guess is taken, the opposing player must tell how many crashes the test word has with his target word. For example, suppose the second player's target word is *hope*. If the first player uses the test word *pots*, player 2 would say "one

Crash (continued)

Number of Players

crash" (the letter *o*). Even though the letter *p* is in both the target and test words, there is no crash because the letters are in different positions. Both players should record the number of crashes beside each guess.

5. Players continue taking turns until one player figures out the other player's target word and uses it as his test word. The first player to figure out his opponent's target word is the winner.

Wordmaster (Jotto)

Number of Players	2
Object	To decode the opponent's secret word before she decodes yours
Materials	pencil for each player paper for each player
Playing the Game	

1. Players divide their papers down the middle with a vertical line. Each player writes a secret, four-letter target word on the line at the top of the right column. Proper nouns are not allowed. Each player then folds the top of the paper down so her opponent can't accidentally see the target word. Players write the letters of the alphabet at the bottoms of their papers.

2. Players decide who will guess first. The first player guesses any four-letter word in the appropriate language. She writes the guess in the left column of her paper. The opponent writes the guess on the right column of her paper beneath her secret word. The opponent should repeat the guess aloud to the first player to ensure the guess has been recorded and spelled correctly.

3. The second player compares the first player's guess with her target word. She then tells the first player the number of letters the two words have in common. The first player records that number in the left column next to her guess. The second player does not tell which letters of the guess are in the target word. The first player has to figure that out.

Wordmaster (Jotto) (continued)

Playing the Game

4. If the first player can eliminate any letters as a result of her guess (if the opponent has told her "zero," for example), she crosses those letters out in the alphabet at the bottom of the paper. Later, when she becomes sure that a certain letter is in the opponent's word, she circles that letter.

5. After the first player has made a guess and recorded the results, the second player makes a guess in the same way. Players take turns until one player, in her turn, guesses the other player's word exactly. The first player to guess the opponent's target word is the winner.

6. Players use logic to figure out their opponent's secret word. They may best do this by making slight changes in their guesses. For example, suppose the first player guesses "barn" and her opponent says "one letter." The first player's next guess might be "burn." If her opponent then tells her "zero letters," she can be certain that the letter *a* is somewhere in her opponent's secret word.

Variation

This game is more difficult and challenging if players use five-letter target words. In that case, all guesses must also be five-letter words.

Oilers

The game is named after Leonhard Euler, the Swiss mathematician.

Number of Players	2
Object	For the "toiler": to collect 4 cards from the group of 16 that share a common suit or face value, or to force the "spoiler" to do so; for the "spoiler": to prevent himself and the toiler from taking any four cards that have a common suit or face value
Materials	paper pencil 16 cards from a standard deck—the ace, two, three, and four of each suit
Playing the Game	1. Players decide who will play first. After the first game, the loser of the previous game plays first. All 16 cards are placed face up on the table. 2. The first player—the "toiler"—claims any 1 card from the array and places the card face up in front of him. 3. The second player—the "spoiler"—claims any 1 of the remaining cards and places it face up in front of him. 4. Players continue alternating turns. The toiler attempts to claim all four cards in any one suit, or all four cards of the same face value. The toiler also wins if the spoiler ends up with a set of four cards matching in either suit or face value. The spoiler wins if neither player has a set of four matching cards at the end of the game. 5. Players reverse roles after each game. The first player to win two games in a row wins the match.

Oilers (continued)

Variation	Parlett's version of the game is played with an array of words such as the following:

ape	day	can	rat
lip	die	tin	rig
hop	dot	one	row
put	bud	sun	rue

In this version, the toiler tries to claim any four words that share a letter or force his opponent to do so. The spoiler tries to prevent either player from claiming a set of four words that share a letter.

Modified from a game, credited to Dave Silverman in *Word Ways,* from David Parlett's *Botticelli and Beyond: Over 100 of the World's Best Word Games,* New York, Pantheon Books, 1981. Used with permission.

Matrix

Number of Players	Any number
Object	To make as many words as possible in a matrix using letters chosen by the players
Materials	copies of choice of game board (pages 139, 140, and 141) pencils or pens a good dictionary
Playing the Game	1. Matrix may be played on a 4-by-4, 5-by-5, or 6-by-6 square grid. Players decide which grid to use before the game begins.

2. In turn, each player calls out a letter. When a letter is called, all players must write it in one of the squares of their own matrices. Players should try to place the letter so that it will help make words in the grid. Once a letter has been placed on the grid, it may not be moved. When it is a player's turn to call a letter, she should first make sure that other players have finished placing the previous letter. Players should call letters that will be most helpful to themselves. However, every player must use each letter somewhere in the grid, whether or not it helps her build words.

3. Only words written from left to right or from top to bottom score points.

4. There is no limit to the number of times any one letter of the alphabet may be used in a game.

5. The last remaining square is a free space. Each player may fill in that square with a letter of her choice.

Matrix (continued)

Playing the Game

6. Scoring is calculated according to the following point system after the final square of the matrix is filled:

two-letter words	=	**3 points**
three-letter words	=	**5 points**
four-letter words	=	**10 points**
five-letter words	=	**20 points**
six-letter words	=	**30 points**

Players list all the words they have made either across or down. If the same word has been made more than once, it counts for a score as often as it has been made.

7. When a large group plays Matrix, one person may serve as recorder. As each letter is called, the recorder writes it on a blackboard or chart paper. This step helps players keep track of which letters have been called.

Game Board: 5-Block Square Grid

Game Board: 6-Block Square Grid

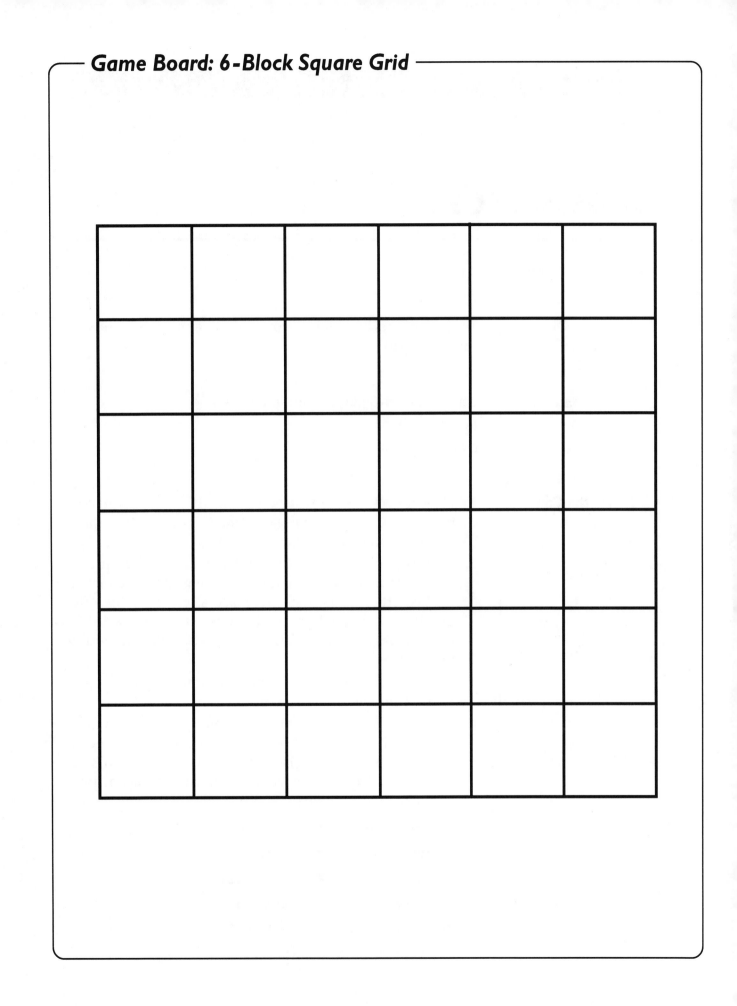

Crosswords

Number of Players	2 to 4
Object	To score points by making words of three or more letters in the game grid
Materials	copies of 8-by-8 game board (page 144) pencils or pens a dictionary
Playing the Game	1. Players decide who will play first. After the first game, the loser of the previous game plays first. Play then proceeds counterclockwise around the group. 2. In turn, each player writes a letter in one of the squares on the game grid. He then passes the grid to the player on his left. Players may not place a letter on the grid unless they are spelling a real English word, or a word in the language in which they are playing. Proper nouns may not be used. 3. There is no limit to the number of times any one letter of the alphabet may be used. 4. Points are scored each time a player completes a new word of three or more letters. On a separate sheet of paper, each player keeps a running list of the words he makes and their point values, determined according to the following chart:

3-letter words =   3 points
4-letter words =   5 points
5-letter words =   10 points
6-letter words =   20 points
7-letter words =   50 points
8-letter words = 100 points

Crosswords *(continued)*

Playing the Game

5. Only words written either down or from left to right score points. Placement of one letter may result in two words, one across and one down. In that case, both words count for the player's scores.

6. Once a word has been made, other players may add letters at the beginning or end to build longer words and score more points. The same word may be used more than once in the same game.

7. If a player does not believe the preceding player has added a letter that will spell an acceptable word, he may challenge. A player may challenge only when it is his turn. In case of a challenge, the preceding player must state the word he is spelling. If he is not spelling an acceptable word, the player who issued the challenge adds ten points to his score. But if the challenged player does have a real word in mind, he adds ten points to his score, and the challenger must subtract ten points. In case of disagreement, the chosen dictionary will determine whether a word scores.

8. The game is over when all squares in the grid are filled, or when players agree than no more words can be made.

Variation

Each player starts the game with a game grid. Each player writes a letter and passes his grid to the left. Each player adds a letter to the new grid, and then passes it on again. Each player keeps a list of every word he makes and its score. Players may want to limit each turn to one minute in this version of the game.

Game Board: Crosswords

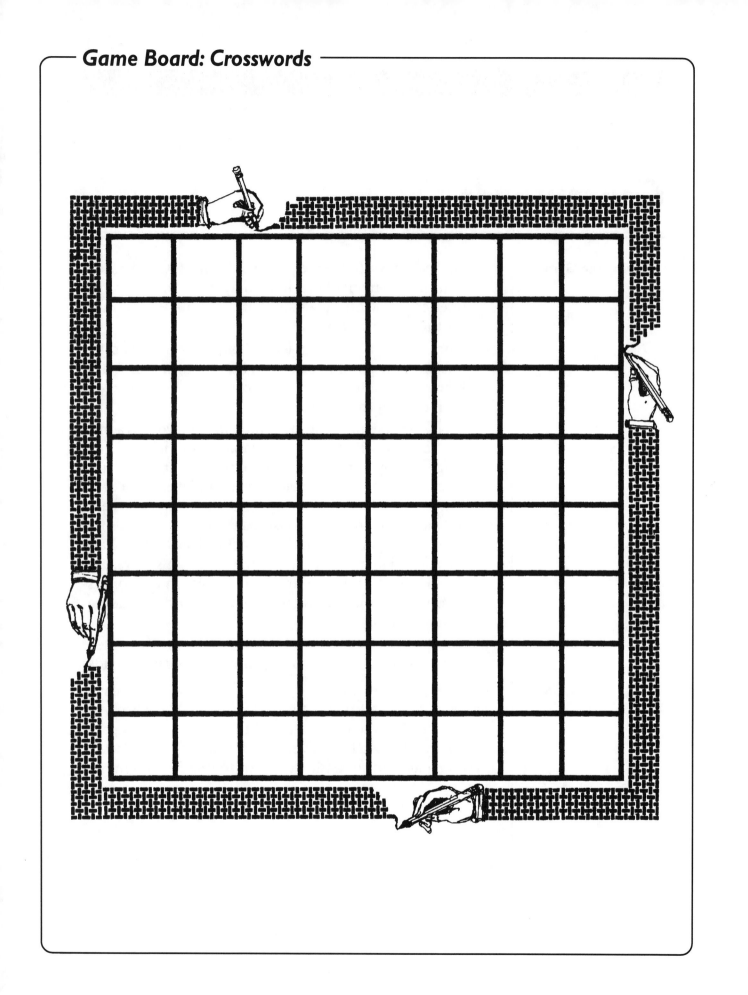

Ghost

Number of Players	2 to 8
Object	To avoid adding a letter that completes a word
Materials	dictionary paper pencil

Playing the Game

1. Players sit in a circle. Play proceeds clockwise around the circle.

2. The first player calls out a letter. The player to her left adds a letter. In turn, each player adds another letter until a word of 4 or more letters is completed.

3. Players must be spelling a real word when they add a letter (unless they are bluffing). They need not be spelling the same word the previous player had in mind. Players try to avoid finishing a word.

4. Proper nouns may not be used. Words of three letters or fewer do not count. A dictionary serves as judge if disputes about words arise.

5. If a player completes a word, she loses a round of the game. A player loses even if she unintentionally spells a word she had not thought of. Each time a player loses a round she is assigned the next letter in the word *ghost*. She gets a *g* when she loses the first time, then an *h, o, s,* and *t* in subsequent losses. When a player has lost five times, thus spelling *ghost,* she is eliminated from the game.

Ghost *(continued)*

Playing the Game

6. If a player thinks the previous player is not spelling an acceptable word or is spelling a word incorrectly, she may challenge. A player may challenge only when it is her turn. The player who is challenged must reveal the word she is spelling. If she is spelling an acceptable word correctly, the challenger loses the round and gets a letter. But if the challenged player is not spelling an acceptable word or is spelling it incorrectly, then she loses and gets a letter.

7. When a player has spelled a complete word, that round of play ends. A challenge also ends a round of play. The player immediately to the left of the player who ended the round—either by finishing a word or challenging—starts the next round with the first letter of a new word. Play continues until all players but one have been eliminated.

Variations
(for experts only)

1. You may make the game more difficult by requiring the minimum length of a word to be 5 or 6 letters rather than 4.

2. SuperGhost: In SuperGhost, all the rules of Ghost apply, except players may add letters to either end of the word.

3. SuperDuperGhost: All rules of Ghost apply, except players may add letters anywhere in the word, as long as they do not change the order of letters.

Madword

Number of Players	4 to 10
Object	To score the most points by making words with Scrabble tiles
Materials	paper for each player pencil for each player set of Scrabble tiles 3-minute timer dictionary
Playing the Game	

1. Each player draws ten Scrabble tiles from a bag or box, without looking. Each player writes his name at the upper right corner of a sheet of paper. Players then record the ten letters—and their point values—at the top of their papers.

2. One player serves as timekeeper. The timekeeper starts the 3-minute timer. Each player writes down as many different words as he can make with the ten letters. Players write the score of each word beside it. If they wish, players may manipulate the letter tiles as they think. As in other word games, players may not use proper nouns, contractions, acronyms, or abbreviations.

3. When time is up, each player draws a line on his paper beneath the words he made. Players then add the total score of their words and record them on separate sheets of paper.

4. Players then pass their papers, along with the letter tiles, to their left. Each player signs his initials below the line that the previous player drew. The timekeeper starts the timer again. Each player makes new words with the letters at the top of the page and records the score of each word. Players may not use words that have been written by the previous player.

Madword (continued)

Playing the Game

5. When time expires, players tally their scores and add them to their previous scores. Each player draws another line under his words and passes the sheet once more.

6. Players have three more minutes to make additional words using the letters on the paper. Words that have already been written may not be used. After three minutes, scoring is done as before.

7. After the third round, papers are turned over or discarded. Each player selects a new set of ten letters and play begins again.

8. Play continues until one player reaches 500 points or some other agreed-upon total.

Snagaram (Anagrams)

Number of Players	2 or more
Object	To be the first to unscramble the letters to form a real word
Materials	paper for each player pencil for each player
Playing the Game	1. Players sit in a circle. Each player thinks of a 5-letter word. She then writes the letters of that word on her paper in scrambled order.
	2. In unison, each player passes her paper to the player on her left. Each player tries to unscramble the letters to form an acceptable English word (or a word in the language in which the game is being played) as quickly as possible. As soon as a player has written the word on the paper, she calls out "Snagaram!" The first player to call out and have the word correct is the winner of that round. The first player to win five rounds wins the match.
Variation	Players may decide to use 6- or 7-letter words to make play more difficult.

Anagrammer

Number of Players	2 to 10
Object	To score points by adding letters to make longer and longer words
Materials	Scrabble tiles paper for each player pencil for each player 1-minute timer
Playing the Game	

1. Players choose someone to serve as timekeeper. Each player picks two Scrabble tiles and writes the letters on his paper.
2. Using the two letters from the tiles and any two additional letters, each player makes a four-letter word. Players write the words on their papers. Each player writes his initials beside the word he has made.
3. Players then pass their papers to the left. The timekeeper starts the timer. Players have one minute either to rearrange the letters to make an anagram of the word already on the paper, or to add one additional letter, then arrange the letters in any order to make a new word.
4. Each player writes his initials beside the new word.
5. When time is called, players record their scores and pass papers to the left. Once again, each player may either add one more letter and rearrange letters to make a new word, or simply make a new anagram using just the letters of the word already on the paper.
6. There is no limit to the number of times any one letter of the alphabet may be used.

Anagrammer (continued)

Playing the Game

7. Players score one point for each letter in each word they make. Players keep their own scores as the papers travel around the group.

8. If a player is unable to make a new word or anagram, he scores no points. The player simply passes the paper on at the end of the minute. A round of play is over when none of the players may produce a new word or anagram. The player with the highest score at the end of the game is the winner.

Wordbuilder

Number of Players	2 to 8
Object	To build the longest word in a series of anagrams
Materials	paper for each player pencil for each player 1-minute timer dictionary

Playing the Game

1. Players arrange themselves around a table. One player serves as timekeeper. Each player writes her name at the top of a sheet of paper.

2. One player, serving as game leader, calls out any three-letter word. The timekeeper then starts a timer.

3. All players write that word on their papers. Each player then uses the three letters in that word and any one additional letter to make a four-letter word. Letters may be rearranged in any manner.

4. Proper nouns may not be used. There is no limit to the number of times any one letter of the alphabet may be used.

5. After one minute, each player writes her initials next to the word she has made. Each player then passes her paper to the left. The timekeeper restarts the timer. Players add one additional letter to the word they received and rearrange the letters to form a five-letter word. Each player writes her initials beside the word she makes.

6. Players continue passing the pieces of paper around the table at one-minute intervals. After each pass, each player adds another letter to the word on the sheet and creates a new anagram—if she can.

Wordbuilder (continued)

Playing the Game

7. A round of play is over when no player can make a new word within one minute. Players then pass the papers back to their right. Each player writes down the number of letters in the words she has made as the papers pass back by her. She tallies her own score when she receives the paper she began. A player gets one point for each letter in each anagram she produced. For example, a player may have made one six-letter word, two five-letter words, and a four-letter word. That player's score for that round would be 20.

8. After everyone has tallied and recorded their scores, the player to the left of the first game leader calls out a new three-letter word to begin the next round of play. The player with the highest score at the end of the game is the winner.

99 Syllables

Number of Players	Any number
Object	To reassemble a list of syllables into the words from which they came
Materials	paper for each player pencil for each player 15-minute timer
Playing the Game	1. The game leader thinks of a number of interesting words with a total of 99 syllables. The leader then separates the words into syllables and writes the syllables in alphabetical order on a sheet of chart paper. Or the leader may write the syllables on a sheet of 8 1/2-by-11-inch paper that can reproduced so each player will have a copy. 2. To begin play, the game leader displays the list of 99 syllables or gives each player a copy of the list. The leader then starts the timer. Players have fifteen minutes (or some other agreed-upon amount of time) to assemble the syllables into words. 3. After time has expired, the leader reads out the original list of words in alphabetical order. The leader also announces the number of syllables in each word. Players score one point for each syllable they reassembled into a word the leader had on the original list. The player with the highest point total is the winner.
Variation	To make the game easier, it may be played with a smaller number of total syllables—50 or 25, for example.

This game was created by Martin Fleisher Meenakshisundaram and is used with his permission.

In-Words *(Version 1)*

Number of Players	3 or more
Object	To make the longest possible words that include selected three-letter words
Materials	paper for each player pencil for each player blackboard or chart paper 15-minute timer
Playing the Game	1. Players generate a list of ten two- and three-letter words. Someone writes the words on a blackboard or piece of chart paper so that everyone can see them. Each word in the list must be a real, English word, or a word in the language in which you are playing. Proper nouns are not allowed.

2. One player serves as timekeeper. Players have 15 minutes (or some other agreed-upon amount of time) to think of the longest words that incorporate the ten short words, one long word per short word.

3. Each short word must be included within the larger word with the letters in order and unseparated by other letters. For example, if one of the short words is *bet,* then the word *alphabetical* is acceptable, but *beautiful* is not.

4. When time is called, players share their responses. Players score a point for each letter in each of the large words they thought of. Each player may use only one large scoring word for each of the ten original short words. The player with the highest total score is the winner.

5. In cases of dispute, consult the chosen dictionary.

In-Words *(Version 2)*

Number of Players	3 or more
Object	To make the longest list of words that include a selected three-letter word
Materials	paper for each player pencil for each player 3-minute timer

Playing the Game

1. Players agree on any common three-letter word. Each player writes the word at the top of his paper.

2. One player volunteers to serve as timekeeper. At the timekeeper's signal, players begin writing as many five-letter or longer words as they can think of that contain the three-letter word. For example, suppose the chosen word is *and.* Players may write words such as *sandwich, andiron, handkerchief, ampersand,* and so on.

3. Each three-letter word must be included within the larger word with the letters in order and unseparated by other letters. Using the example above, words such as *anadromous* or *palindrome* are not allowed.

4. Players have three minutes to write as many words as they can think of that incorporate the chosen three-letter word. At the end of that time, the player with the largest number of acceptable words is the winner.

Prefixes

Number of Players	Any number
Object	To list the 10 longest words beginning with a certain prefix
Materials	paper for each player pencil for each player dictionary
Playing the Game	1. One player volunteers to serve as timekeeper. Players agree on a certain prefix to use for the game. There are, of course, many to choose from: *un, uni, con, dis, sub, in, pro, bi, re, over,* and so on. 2. At the timekeeper's signal, players have ten minutes (or some other agreed-upon period) to write the five longest words they can think of that begin with the chosen prefix. Each player records her words on her own paper. 3. When time is called, each player reads her five words. Players get one point for each letter in each of the words. Players get an additional point for each word on their list that no one else thought of. In checking the score, players must be sure the words begin with the actual prefix and not simply the letters of the prefix. For example, if the prefix is *un, uncontrollable* is an acceptable answer, but *uniformity, understanding,* and *undulation* are not.
Variation	The identical game may be played with suffixes or with root words.

Modified from a game found in David Parlett's *Botticelli and Beyond: Over 100 of the World's Best Word Games*, New York, Pantheon Books, 1981. Used with permission.

Backwords and Forewords

Number of Players	Any number
Object	To make the two longest words starting and ending with selected letters
Materials	Scrabble tiles paper for each player pencil for each player 2-minute timer dictionary
Playing the Game	1. One player volunteers to be timekeeper or game leader. That player draws two tiles at random, without looking.

Playing the Game

1. One player volunteers to be timekeeper or game leader. That player draws two tiles at random, without looking.

2. The game leader announces the two tiles to the rest of the players. Players write the two letters on their papers.

3. Players then have two minutes to write the longest possible words they can think of that begin and end with the two chosen letters. For example, if the two letters selected were *r* and *g,* a player might make the words *reducing* and *gardener.*

4. Proper nouns are not allowed. In case of disputes, players should consult the chosen dictionary.

5. Players score one point for each letter in each of the two words.

6. The next player chooses two new tiles and players try to form two new words. Play continues for an agreed-upon number of rounds. The player with the highest score at the end of the game is the winner.

Acrostics

Number of Players	2 or more
Object	To think of the longest possible words beginning and ending with particular letters
Materials	paper for each player pencil for each player dictionary 10-minute timer
Playing the Game	1. Players choose any word containing six letters or more.
	2. Each player writes the word vertically down the left side of his paper. Each player then writes the word again, backward, down the right side of his paper. For example, if the word chosen is *because,* each player's paper should look like this:

B   **E**

E   **S**

C   **U**

A   **A**

U   **C**

S   **E**

E   **B**

Acrostics *(continued)*

Playing the Game

3. Players get ten minutes (or some other agreed-upon amount of time) to write the longest words they can think of that begin and end with these letters. In our example, players would have to think of the longest word that begins with *b* and ends with *e,* then the longest word that begins with *e* and ends with *s,* and so on. Proper nouns may not be used.

4. When time is called, players share their words and count the number of letters in each. In case of challenges, players consult the chosen dictionary. Each letter counts for one point. The player with the highest total is the winner.

Variations

1. If players choose, they may use dictionaries as references while they play the game. This makes the game less competitive, but turns it into an interesting vocabulary builder.

2. Instead of using the letters of a single word to start and end their words, players write the entire alphabet down the left and right sides of their paper. The alphabet on the right side of the paper may be written either in alphabetical order or reverse alphabetical order, or the letters on the right side may be written in alphabetical order starting with a letter other than *a.* After writing the letter *z,* players simply continue with *a, b, c,* and so on until all letters of the alphabet are used.

Acrosticals

Number of Players	Any number
Object	To make the longest words beginning with the letters of a ten-letter word
Materials	paper for each player pencil for each player timer
Playing the Game	1. Players agree on any ten-letter word to use as the key word. Players also choose a timekeeper and agree on a time limit for play—ten minutes is a reasonable amount of time. 2. Each player writes the key word across the top of her paper. The players then attempt to make the longest possible word beginning with each letter of the key word, using only the letters contained in the key word. 3. If a certain letter appears only once in the key word, it may be used only once in each of the scoring words. If it appears twice in the key word, it may be used twice, and so on. However, a player must use a different scoring word for each use of the same letter. For example, let's suppose the key word is *catalogues*. One player's paper might look like this:

Clogs	**Least**	**Use**
Ascot	**Oats**	**Eats**
Talc	**Guest**	**Stale**
Agues		

4. Neither the key word itself, nor truncated (cut off) portions of it may be used as scoring words. For example, using the key word *catalogues*, a player may not use *catalogue, catalog,* or even *cat* or *log* to score points.

5. When time is called, players announce the words they have made. Players score one point for each letter in each word, with the highest score winning.

Source: Gyles Brandreth, referred to in David Parlett's *Botticelli and Beyond: Over 100 of the World's Best Word Games,* New York, Pantheon Books, 1981. Used with permission.

Sentences

Also known as Telegram

Number of Players	2 or more
Object	To form as many sentences as possible from words beginning with the letters of a chosen word
Materials	paper for each player pencil for each player 2-minute timer
Playing the Game	1. One player chooses a key word of four letters or more. Each player writes the word down on a piece of paper. The player who chose the word serves as timekeeper for the round.
	2. At the timekeeper's signal, players have 2 minutes (or some other agreed-upon length of time) to make as many sentences as possible with words that start with the letters of the key word. For example, if the key word is *paper*, a player might write *Paul ate pickled eggs repeatedly* or *Proud Americans prefer equal rights*.
	3. When time is up, players read their sentences to the group. A player scores one point for each sentence completed within the time limit. Only complete, grammatically correct sentences count for scores.
	4. The next player then chooses a different word and begins the next round of play.
	5. At the end of the agreed-upon number of rounds, or after each player has chosen the key word, the players tally up their scores. The player with the highest score wins the game.

Source: Jack Maguire's *Hopscotch, Hangman, Hot Potato, and Ha Ha Ha,* New York, Prentice Hall, 1990. Used with permission.

Word Train

Number of Players	2 to 8
Object	To continue a series of words for as long as possible
Materials	any book paper for each player pencil for each player 1-minute timer

Playing the Game

1. Players sit in a circle. One player volunteers to serve as time-keeper. In turn, each player opens a book (any book will do) to a page at random. Without looking, players point somewhere on the page and write the individual words they've pointed to on their papers. The book is passed around the circle until each player has written down a word.

2. The timekeeper then starts a 1-minute timer. Players use the last two letters of the individual words they have written as the first two letters of new words. They write the new words below the words they pointed to in the book.

3. When time expires, players pass their papers to the left. Any player who has not thought of a new word within the time limit drops out of the round.

4. The timekeeper restarts the timer, and players again have one minute to make new individual words beginning with the last two letters of the words their opponents have created.

5. If a player cannot create an acceptable word within the time limit, he is eliminated from the game. Play continues around the circle until all but one player has been eliminated. The remaining player is the winner of that round of the game. All players rejoin the game to start the next round.

Variation

This game may be played noncompetitively, starting with a single word. All players work together to extend the train for as long as possible.

Word Ladders

Number of Players	Any number
Object	To change a word one letter at a time, transforming it into a completely different word in the fewest number of steps
Materials	paper for each player pencil for each player dictionaries
Playing the Game	1. The game leader chooses a pair of four- or five-letter words. The words may be related in some way to provide added interest, although they need not be.
	2. Each player tries to transform the first word of the pair into the second by changing one letter at a time, making an acceptable word each step, ending with the second word. For example, if the leader chose *mind* and *body*, a player would change the *m* in *mind* to *b* to make *bind*, then the *i* to *o* to make *bond*, then the *d* to *y* to make *bony*, finally changing the *n* to *d* to make *body*. If the two words were *heat* and *cold*, the player may make the following words in order: *heat, head, held, hold*, ending with the second word, *cold*.
	3. Each step in the ladder must be a real English word, or a word in the language in which players are playing. Players may use dictionaries as they build their word ladders.
	4. The player who makes the transformation with the fewest number of steps is the winner.

Categories

Number of Players	3 or more
Object	To think of a word in each category that no other player thinks of
Materials	paper pencil Scrabble tiles 5-minute timer
Playing the Game	1. As a group, players make up a list of ten categories—authors, colors, countries, girls' names, boys' names, items of clothing, and so on. Each player writes her categories on a sheet of paper. 2. One of the players agrees to serve as timekeeper. The timekeeper chooses a letter at random by drawing a Scrabble tile without looking. The timekeeper announces the letter to the group, then starts a 5-minute timer. 3. Each player tries to think of a word starting with the chosen letter that fits in each category. Players write their words on their sheets of paper. 4. At the end of five minutes, players announce the words they've thought of in each category. A player scores 2 points for any acceptable word that no one else has thought of. If more than one player has written the same word, each player scores one point. The player with the highest total score is the winner.

Guggenheim

Number of Players	Any number
Object	To fill in all the cells of the game grid with appropriate items
Materials	paper for each player pencil for each player 5-minute timer
Playing the Game	1. Each player draws a 5-by-5 grid on a piece of paper. The group then chooses five categories of common things or people. These could be anything: chemical elements, famous musicians, flowers, presidents, countries of the world, and so on. The players write the five categories along the left sides of their grids. 2. A player then chooses a five-letter key word. Each player writes the key word across the top of the grid. 3. Each player then has five minutes (or some other agreed-upon time) to fill in the grid with words in each category that start with the letters of the key word. For example, let's suppose the key word is *horse*. One player's grid might look like the following grid:

	H	**O**	**R**	**S**	**E**
elements	helium	oxygen		selenium	
musicians	Hayden		Rubenstein	Sting	Elvis
flowers	hollyhocks	oleander	rose	snapdragon	
presidents	Hoover		Roosevelt		Eisenhower
countries	Haiti		Romania		Estonia

4. When time expires, players share their responses. Players get two points for each item that no other player has listed, and one point for any entry that someone else has also written. Empty cells score no points. The player with the highest score wins.

Word Chains

Number of Players	Any number
Object	To make as long a chain of associated words as possible
Materials	paper pencils or pens—*or* chalkboard chalk
Playing the Game	1. One player—the game leader—writes a common word on a blackboard or piece of paper. Players then think of another word that is commonly associated with the first in a phrase. The game leader then writes that word after the first word. 2. Players continue working cooperatively to add words to the chain. Each word should form a common phrase or compound word with the word immediately preceding it. For example, if the leader chooses *hot,* the group may think of *dog* for *hot dog.* The players may then come up with *house* for *doghouse, paint* for *house paint, brush* for *paintbrush,* and so on. 3. Players build the word chain until they come to a dead end and can think of nothing else to add. They then count the number of words in the chain and try to improve on that score in the next round of the game.
Variation	Players may try to build a word circle by bringing their chain back to connect with the original word.

Pun-Dits

Number of Players	Any number
Object	To create the best pun in answer to a question
Materials	paper for each player pencil for each player
Playing the Game	1. As a group, players create a list of ten diverse professions or specific personal traits, for example, *athlete, doctor, politician, musician, banker, farmer,* and so on. 2. Players then agree on a question to be answered for each of these people, for example, "Where would a _____ go on vacation?" "What kind of car would a _____ drive?" or "What is a _____ 's favorite food?" 3. Players separate for five minutes. Each player tries to think of the best pun to answer the question for each of the ten people on the list, for example, "Where would a banker go on vacation?" "The Czech Republic." "What kind of a car would a farmer drive?" "A chicken coupe." "What is a musician's favorite food?" "Fish, because of the scales." No one is expected to come up with answers to all ten. 4. The group gets back together and shares their answers. No scoring is necessary. This game is just for fun.

Hink Pink

Number of Players	Any number
Object	To score points by guessing the correct rhyming answer to other players' questions
Materials	paper for each player pencil for each player rhyming dictionaries thesauruses
Playing the Game	

1. Each player creates and writes down three hink-pinks, hinky-pinkies, or hinkety-pinketies. A *hink-pink* is a riddle answered with two rhyming one-syllable words. For example, "What is an old, beat-up trumpet?" "A worn horn." "What is a domestic rodent?" "A house mouse." A *hinky-pinky* uses two rhyming two-syllable words in the answer. For example, "What is a happy canine?" "A jolly collie." "What is someone who makes noise with laboratory glassware?" "A beaker squeaker." *Hinkety-pinketies* are harder. They use answers of two rhyming three-syllable or more words. For example, "What does a sled dog need when he jumps out of a plane?" "A malamute parachute." "How does a Japanese warrior put his baby to sleep?" "With a Samurai lullaby." Players must keep their papers hidden from one another.

2. Players sit in a circle. In turn, each player asks a riddle. The first person to shout out an answer gets a point.

3. Play continues around the circle three times until all players have had a chance to ask all three of the riddles they have created. Players then tally the points they have earned. The player with the most points is the winner.

Tom Swifties

Number of Players	2 teams of 3 or more
Object	To figure out as many of the opposing team's Tom Swifties and croakers as possible
Materials	paper for each team pencil for each team dictionaries timer

Playing the Game

1. Players divide into two equal teams. The teams separate so that they cannot overhear each other. One member of each team volunteers to serve as timekeeper.

2. Each team creates a group of five Tom Swifties or croakers. A *Tom Swifty* is a pun using adverbs written into a sentence. For example, "'It's time to feed the hogs,' Tom said sloppily." "'All right, who turned off the lights?'" Tom asked excitedly" (ex-sightedly). "'We're going on a camping trip,' Tom said intensely" (in tents ly). "'I called last time,' Tom said euphoniously" (You phone iously). A *Croaker* is a similar kind of pun using a verb. For example, "'That's not my dog,' Tom muttered." "'This weighs exactly one sixteenth of a pound,' Tom announced."

3. Each team writes its Tom Swifties and Croakers on five separate slips of paper, leaving a blank for the punning verb or adverb. For example, one of the first team's slips might read, "'Would you like to buy some trout?' Tom asked _____." (*Selfishly* is the answer for the example.)

Tom Swifties *(continued)*

Playing the Game

4. After the teams have finished writing, they rejoin. Teams take turns drawing the slips of paper and attempting to complete the puns. Teams have two minutes to complete each Tom Swifty and Croaker. A member of the other team starts timing as soon as the paper is drawn, and stops when someone on the opposing team says the correct answer.

5. The timekeeper records the number of seconds the opposing team takes to complete the Tom Swifty or Croaker. If the team cannot answer, the timekeeper writes down a score of 120 seconds, and someone from the opposing team reveals the correct answer.

6. Play alternates between teams until each team has tried to answer all five puns. At the end of the game, the team that has used the least amount of time to complete all five is the winner.

Dictionary

Number of Players	6 to 20
Object	To score points by identifying the real definition of an unusual word, or by fooling other players with your false definition
Materials	dictionary 3-by-5-inch cards (or small squares of paper) pencils or pens
Playing the Game	1. Players choose someone to serve as game leader. Leadership rotates among the players as the game continues. Each player writes his name at the top of the 3-by-5-inch card.
	2. The game leader finds an unusual word in the dictionary, one he thinks no one will know. He announces the word. If any of the other players know the word, they must say so. The leader continues to search until he finds a word that no one knows.
	3. The leader spells and pronounces the unfamiliar word to the other players. Each player writes the word on a card. The leader does not tell the players what the word means or what part of speech it is.
	4. Each player then creates an imaginary definition for the word and writes it on the card. Players try to make their definitions sound as real as possible. Players hide their definitions so no one else sees them. The leader writes the actual definition on a separate card.
	5. When players are finished writing, the leader collects all cards. He shuffles the cards, including the card with the real definition, and reads them to the players one at a time. As they listen, players try to identify the real definition.

Dictionary (continued)

Playing the Game

6. The leader reads the definitions a second time. This time, players vote for the definition they think is the real one. Each player votes only once. Players may not vote for their own definitions. The leader records the number of votes for each definition on its card.

7. After everyone has voted, the leader announces the actual definition. The leader also announces who wrote the false definitions that received votes, and how many votes each one received. A player gets one point for each vote that his phony definition got from other players. A player also gets a point if he voted for the actual definition.

8. A new game leader is then chosen for the next round. The player who has the most points when the group agrees to end the game is the winner.

Adverbs

Number of Players	3 or more
Object	For a person to guess the adverb that the other players have chosen
Materials	none
Playing the Game	1. One player leaves the room. The other players agree on an adverb—a word that describes how something is done, such as *quickly, carefully, furtively, joyfully, angrily, powerfully, gently, lovingly.*
	2. The person is then brought back into the room. She asks individual players to perform a variety of actions in the manner of the adverb. For example, she might say "Susan, sing in the manner of the adverb" or "Bob, walk across the room in the manner of the adverb."
	3. After each performance, she tries to guess the adverb. Play continues until she guesses the word or gives up.

Questions

Number of Players	2
Object	To carry on a conversation consisting only of questions
Materials	none
Playing the Game	

1. Players agree on who will play first. After the first game, the loser of the previous game plays first. The first player begins the round of conversation with any question.

2. The second player must then respond—appropriately—with another question. The conversation continues back and forth between the two players until one either answers with a statement, repeats a question that has already been used in that round, uses a question that is a non sequitur (does not follow from the previous question), answers with a rhetorical question—a statement in question form (example: don't you think it's a beautiful day?), or is unable to respond at all. A round of play might go something like the following:

   Player 1: *Do you think it will rain?*

   Player 2: *Do you think it will hail?*

   Player 1: *Why? Are you worried about your garden?*

   Player 2: *Did something I said make you think so?*

   Player 1: *When did you last water your garden?*

   Player 2: *Why do you care so much about my garden?*

   Player 1: *Because I enjoy eating your tomatoes . . . oops!*

   Player 2 wins this point. For a much more amusing example, find a copy of Tom Stoppard's play *Rosencrantz and Guildenstern Are Dead,* from which this game is taken.

3. Stoppard's characters use a four-point system, scoring like a tennis match (Love, 15, 30, 40, Game), which seems as good a method as any.

Dumb Crambo

Number of Players	6 or more
Object	To guess the other team's secret word in the fewest tries
Materials	none
Playing the Game	

1. Players divide into two teams. Each team goes into a separate room and chooses a secret word, one with many other words that rhyme with it.

2. The two teams then join each other. Players decide which team will play first. The players on the first team say, "We're looking for a word that rhymes with _____" (a word that rhymes with their secret word). For example, if their secret word is *light*, they might say, "We're looking for a word that rhymes with *night*."

3. Members of the other team are not allowed to speak. In turn, they silently act out rhyming words, until someone on the team finds the secret word. For example, they might gnash their teeth. The first team would then say, "No, it's not *bite*." Then one could pantomime throwing punches, and the first team would respond "No, it's not *fight*." The first team keeps count of the number of words their opponents act out before they get the secret word. Actions that the other team can't interpret still count as attempts. If a team member forgets and speaks, that also costs the team a point.

4. Once the pantomiming team has guessed the first team's secret word or given up, the roles are reversed.

5. The team that guesses the secret word in the fewest number of pantomimes is the winner of that round. Teams then separate again and choose two new secret words.

Charades   *The classic parlor game*

Number of Players	10 or more
Object	To pantomime the secret title or phrase and have your team guess it as quickly as possible
Materials	slips of paper 2 small containers pens or pencils stopwatch

Playing the Game

1. Players divide into two teams and separate. Each team writes about twenty (or the same number as there are team members) titles of books, movies, TV shows, plays, or songs on individual slips of paper. They may also include short, well-known quotations if both teams agree to do so. Each slip of paper is folded in half and placed in a small container. At least two members of the team must have heard of each item.

2. The teams then join each other. Each team sits in a row, with the two rows facing each another. The first member of one team draws one of the slips of paper from the container that the other team has prepared. That team member reads the slip, but keeps the paper hidden from his teammates and does not speak to them.

3. The team member who has drawn the slip stands facing his own teammates. He has two minutes or other agreed-upon time to pantomime the title or quotation to his own teammates. The rest of the team tries to guess it as quickly as possible. One of the members of the other team gives the signal to begin and serves as timekeeper. The rest of the other team is simply an audience while the first team tries to figure out the pantomime.

Charades (continued)

Playing the Game

4. To work quickly and efficiently, the pantomime usually follows the format outlined in the next several steps. The player pantomimes what category of item is on the sheet, using the following standardized motions:

Book: *pantomime holding an open book with up-turned hands*

Movie: *pantomime holding a movie camera in front of the eye and wind the film with a circular hand motion*

TV show: *pantomime a square box or TV screen*

Song: *pantomime singing, with open mouth and outspread arms*

Play: *pantomime an actor declaiming on stage with one outstretched arm*

Quotation: *pantomime quotation marks by wiggling two fingers of each hand at shoulder level*

5. The player indicates the number of words in the title or quotation by holding up that number of fingers.

6. The player has two options for the next step: He may either act out the item word by word, or act out the item in its entirety. If he chooses the latter option, he makes a circular motion with both hands in front of his body, indicating that he is acting out the whole idea. He then tries to pantomime the item in such a way that his teammates will recognize it.

7. If he chooses to act out the item word by word, he signals which word he is pantomiming by holding up one finger for the first word, two for the second, and so on. Players might not necessarily start with the first word. It's good strategy to start with a key word that will help teammates recognize the entire item.

Charades *(continued)*

Playing the Game

8. The player then pantomimes the word. When a player guesses correctly, the mime points to him to acknowledge the guess. The team member who guessed correctly should repeat the guess to make sure other teammates have heard it.

9. If necessary, the pantomiming player may break a word into syllables, then act it out syllable by syllable. He indicates this by showing the number of syllables with the fingers of one hand laid across the other forearm.

10. The mime may also act out rhyming words, tugging gently on one ear to signal "sounds like . . . " Teammates guess the initial word, then quickly list as many rhymes as they can until they come upon the correct word.

11. There are several other signals the mime may use: holding the thumb and forefinger of one hand close together indicates a little word (*a, of, the, it,* for example); waving an open hand over the shoulder for past tense; and so on. Teams are welcome to make up additional signals that will help the mime communicate with guessing teammates.

12. The game works best when the team members guess as quickly and as often as they can. The faster they guess, the more likely they will be to find the correct words.

13. The timekeeper stops the timer as soon as the team guesses the entire title or quotation correctly or calls time after two minutes. The timekeeper records the elapsed time in seconds on a sheet of paper.

14. The pantomiming player is not permitted to speak. If he forgets himself and speaks during play, a penalty of 30 seconds (or some other agreed-upon amount of time) is added to the team score.

15. Teams take turns drawing from each other's containers and acting out the titles or quotations on the slips of paper. Each player on the team must take a turn being the mime. At the end of play, the team with the lowest score—the fewest total seconds—is the winner.

No No

Number of Players	2 or more
Object	To extend a list of rhyming words for as long as possible
Materials	none
Playing the Game	1. Players sit in a circle and decide who will play first. After the first game, the loser of the previous game plays first.
	2. The first player thinks of a word that has many rhymes. The player thinks of a word that rhymes with his chosen word, then uses its definition for the chosen word. For example, the first player might choose *day,* think of *hay* as a rhyming word, and say, "A day is an animal feed made of dried grasses."
	3. The second player then figures out the rhyming word the first player had in mind. She must use it in a sentence with the definition of yet another rhyming word. For example, she might say, "No, no, you mean *hay,* which is a theatrical presentation with actors and actresses."
	4. The next player continues the process. She might say, "No, no, you mean *play,* which is a body of water."
	5. Each player has a minute to complete her turn. When a player can't come up with the word that the previous player is thinking of or can't think of another new rhyming word, she is out. Play continues until just one player is left. That player is the winner.

Adapted with permission of Sterling Publishing Co., Inc., New York, N.Y., from *Great Party Games for Grownups* by Phil Wiswell, © 1981 by Sterling Publishing Co., Inc.

Crambo

Number of Players	5 or more
Object	To guess the game leader's secret word
Materials	none
Playing the Game	1. Players sit in a circle. They choose one person to be the first game leader.
	2. The game leader thinks of a secret word. He then says, "I am thinking of a word that rhymes with _____," naming a word that rhymes with his word, not the word itself. For example, if the secret word is *twice,* the leader might say, "I'm thinking of a word that rhymes with *nice."*
	3. Players take turns trying to guess the word by using simple definitions of other rhyming words. For example, the first player might say, "Is it something cold?" The leader must then identify something cold that rhymes with the secret word. So he would say, "No, it's not ice."
	4. If the leader is stumped and can't think of a suitable rhyme, the questioner states the word he was thinking of. That questioner then gets another turn to guess.
	5. Play continues until one of the players guesses the secret word. That player becomes the new leader for the next round.

Teapot or Coffeepot

Number of Players	4 or more
Object	For a person to guess the other players' secret pair of homophones
Materials	none
Playing the Game	1. One player leaves the room. The other players select a pair of homophones (two words that sound alike—*weight* and *wait,* for example).
	2. The person is called back into the room. One of the other players begins the game by speaking a sentence that uses both words. However, the player replaces both words with the word *teapot* (or *coffeepot*). Using the example, the player might say, "I had to *teapot* in line to find out what my *teapot* was."
	3. The person now asks other players questions, using the word *teapot,* in an effort to figure out what the secret pair of words is. When players are asked a question, they must reply using at least one of the secret words—but replacing it with *teapot,* of course. Questioning might go like this: "Gina, did you ever have to *teapot* in school?" "I have to *teapot* every day in the cafeteria." "Bob, do you have a *teapot*?" "My *teapot* is bigger than I'd like it to be."
	4. The person asks questions of players in no particular order. When she thinks she knows the secret words, she may guess. There is no penalty for incorrect guesses. If she is wrong, she simply asks more questions. Players may want to agree on a three- or five-minute time limit.
	5. When the guesser guesses the words or when time is up, players select another person to go outside and play continues with a new pair of homophones.

Uncrash

Number of Players	2 to 4
Object	To be the last player to add a word to the list without "crashing"
Materials	paper pencil dictionary
Playing the Game	1. Players sit in a circle and decide who will play first. After the first game, the loser of the previous game plays first. Play moves clockwise around the group. Players also agree on a certain word length to play with. It's a good idea to start with 3-letter words. Players may use longer words as their skills improve.
	2. The first player writes any word of the agreed-upon length on the paper. All words used in the game must be real, English words, or words in the language in which players are playing; neither abbreviations nor proper nouns are allowed.
	3. The second player then writes a word of the same length directly below the first word. None of the letters in the second word can "crash" with the letters of the first word. A *crash* is defined as the same letter in the same location in two different words. For example, if the first player writes *box*, the second player may write *hat* or *ask*, but not *bat* or *toy* because the *b* in *bat* crashes with the *b* in *box*, and the *o* in *toy* crashes with the *o* in *box*.
	4. The next player must add another word to the list. The new word may not crash with either of the words already on the list. Players continue to add new words. No new word may have any crashes with any of the previous words in the list.

Uncrash (continued)

Playing the Game

5. When one player is unable to think of a new word to add to the list, the round of play is over. The last player who successfully added a word to the list wins the round. That player scores a number of points equal to the number of words in the list. The player who was unable to add to the list then picks a new word to start the next round. Play continues until one player reaches or exceeds 100 or some other agreed-upon target score.

Source: David Parlett's *Botticelli and Beyond: Over 100 of the World's Best Word Games,* New York, Pantheon Books, 1981. Used with permission.

Taboo

Number of Players	2
Object	To force an opponent to say chosen forbidden words while avoiding saying his forbidden words
Materials	paper for each player pencil for each player
Playing the Game	1. Each player writes five common words on a sheet of paper, making sure that the opponent does not see them. Each one of these words is "taboo," or forbidden. Players then turn their papers over.
	2. Players take turns asking one another ten questions. The questions should be designed to force the opponent to speak one of the forbidden words.
	3. In turn, players answer each question with a complete sentence. Each player keeps track of the number of taboo words that his opponent uses in his answers. A player gets two points for each taboo word his opponent used in answering the first five questions, and one point for each taboo word he used in the second five answers. The player with the most points wins.

Taboo Too

Number of Players	6 or more
Object	To figure out the game leader's taboo word
Materials	none
Playing the Game	1. Players sit in a circle and choose someone to be the first game leader. The game leader secretly selects a common word to be the "taboo" word.
	2. The leader asks each player a question in turn. She tries to use questions that will force the player to answer using the taboo word. Players must answer each question with a complete sentence.
	3. If the player uses the word in her answer, the leader says "taboo!" and the player is out of the game until the next round.
	4. Before the leader asks the next player a question, that player gets to guess the taboo word. Play continues around the group, with each player making a guess and then answering another question from the leader if the guess was not correct.
	5. The first player to guess the taboo word correctly becomes the new leader. She chooses a new word and begins the next round of the game.
Variation	Instead of a taboo word, the leader may make a letter of the alphabet taboo. The players must then guess that letter.

Proverbs

Number of Players	4 or more
Object	For a person to guess the proverb that the other players have chosen
Materials	none

Playing the Game

1. The player who is "it" leaves the room. The other players agree on a well-known proverb, such as "A stitch in time saves nine."

2. The person comes back into the room. The other players sit in a circle. "It" begins with any player and goes around the circle asking questions. The first player must use the first word of the proverb somewhere in his answer, the second player must use the second word, and so on. For example, "it" might ask the first player, "What is your favorite sport?" and the first player might answer, "I have always liked a good game of tennis." "It" might then ask the second player, "How are you feeling today?" and the second player could answer, "Not bad, but I have a stitch in my side from running this morning."

3. Play continues around the circle until the last word of the proverb is used in a sentence. The next player to answer a question returns to the first word of the proverb and includes it in the answer again.

4. "It" may use the same question repeatedly—for example, he could ask each person in turn how they are feeling. "It" may guess the proverb at any time, but he only gets three guesses. If the players go through all the words of the proverb three times without "it" guessing correctly, that round of the game is over and "it" loses.

Nymphabet

Number of Players	2
Object	To avoid being the last player to make a word in an alphabetical series
Materials	paper pencil

Playing the Game

1. Players decide who will play first. After the first game, the loser of the previous game plays first. Players may write the alphabet at the top of the paper for reference.

2. The first player writes a word that begins with the letter *a*. Any letters in the word that follow in the alphabet—in order—are eliminated along with the *a*. For example, if the first player were to say *abacus, a, b,* and *c* would be eliminated from the alphabet list. These letters may still be used in other words in the game, but they are not used to begin a word.

3. The second player then writes a word that begins with the letter of the alphabet that follows the last letter eliminated. Continuing our example, the second player must start a word with *d*. Any other letters in that word that follow alphabetically in order are also eliminated. For example, if the second player were to write *definition, d, e,* and *f* would be eliminated.

Nymphabet (continued)

Playing the Game

4. Players continue taking turns until a word eliminates *z*. The player to make the last word is the loser. Following is a sample game:

PLAYER I	PLAYER 2
ABaCus	DEFinition
GHost	IIIness
JacK-o'-Lantern	MoNOPoly
QuaRt	STUmp
VoW	XYlem
Zipper (loses)	

Variations

1. Nymphabet is a better game if the alphabet is thought of as circular—so that after eliminating *z*, players return to *a*. Using this method, the first player starts with any letter of the alphabet. The letter immediately before the starting letter then becomes the last letter in that round of the game. For example, if the first player starts with *hijack*, the final letter becomes *g*, the letter immediately before *h*.

2. Players may keep score by counting the number of letters they eliminate in each turn. In this version of the game, it does not matter who has the last word. The player who eliminates the most letters is the winner. In case of a tie, player 2 is the winner.

Source: David Parlett's *Botticelli and Beyond: Over 100 of the World's Best Word Games*, New York, Pantheon Books, 1981. Used with permission.

Word Sprouts

Invented by
Michael Grendon

Number of Players	2
Object	To score the most points by connecting letters to make words
Materials	paper pencil
Playing the Game	1. One player draws four small circles in a row, connected by arrows pointing from left to right. The players decide who will play first. After the first game, the loser of the previous game plays first. The players then take turns writing a different letter in each circle so that they spell out any four-letter word (see figure 10).

Figure 10. Beginning of Word Sprouts

2. The actual game now begins. The first player draws another circle anywhere on the paper, and writes in it any letter of the alphabet that has not yet been used. The player then draws arrows to connect any letters that form new words (see figure 11).

Figure 11. Next move in Word Sprouts

Word Sprouts (continued)

Playing the Game

3. In turn, each player adds a new letter to the diagram, adding arrows to indicate any new words that have been made. A player must make at least one new word in each turn. There are no limits to the number of different words a player may make in any one turn. Players score one point for each letter of each new word they make.

4. Once a letter has four arrows connected to it, it is "full." No more arrows may be drawn to or from it. It still may be used in new words, however, by using the existing arrows. Players may draw a small *x* beside each full letter to remind them it may have no more new connections.

5. No connecting arrow may cross another. No letter of the alphabet may be used more than once in a game.

6. No pair of letters may be connected by more than one arrow. Arrows may go in one direction only.

7. Players score points only for words that contain their new letter—they may not score with words that the previous player may have overlooked. Each player keeps a list of all the words she has made during the game.

8. Smaller words contained within larger ones do not score additional points. For example, if a player makes the word *masked,* she scores 6 points. There are no additional points for *ask, asked,* or *mask.*

9. If one player cannot make a move, she must pass and give the other player an opportunity. When neither player can make a move, the game is over, and each player tallies her points to determine the winner.

Source: David Parlett's *Botticelli and Beyond: Over 100 of the World's Best Word Games,* New York, Pantheon Books, 1981. Used with permission.

Ingredients

Number of Players	2 teams of 3 or more
Object	To identify the most foods by their lists of ingredients
Materials	3-by-5-inch cards pencil
Playing the Game	1. In advance, players divide into teams. To prepare for the game, each player writes a complete list of ingredients for 3 different food products from their kitchen at home. Each list of ingredients should be typed or written neatly on a separate 3-by-5-inch card. Players do not write the name of the food on the card. However, they should identify each card with their initials and a number, and write the names of the three foods on a separate card. 2. Players agree to the amount of time they will use to figure out the foods. The more people playing, the more time players will need. One player volunteers to serve as timekeeper. A player from each team gathers all the cards from his team. 3. Play begins when the teams exchange cards. Each team tries to identify as many of the foods as they can in the time allotted. The team that identifies the most foods correctly is the winner.

Adapted with permission of Sterling Publishing Co., Inc., New York, N.Y. from *Great Party Games for Grownups* by Phil Wiswell, © 1981 by Sterling Publishing Co., Inc.

Grandmother's Attic

Number of Players	2 or more
Object	To remember everything that has been added to a list
Materials	none

Playing the Game

1. Players sit in a circle. The first player thinks of something that begins with the letter *a* and uses that word in the following sentence: "My grandmother's attic has _____ in it."

2. The player to the left of the first player left then repeats what the first player said, and adds something that starts with a *b*. If the first player said *artichokes,* for example, then the second player might say, "My grandmother's attic has artichokes and a basketball in it."

3. Play continues clockwise around the circle until someone makes a mistake. Then players start all over again.

Variations

1. Add a rule that players are not allowed to laugh (impossible after a while).

2. Play "I am going on a trip." Each player must add a new geographical location, in alphabetical order, after repeating all the places that have already been named.

3. To increase the difficulty, each player must name both a place they are going and an object they will take with them. For example, the first player might say, "I'm going to *Alabama* and I'm taking an *aardvark* with me." The second player might then say, "I'm going to *Alabama* and I'm taking an *aardvark*. Then I'm going to *Boston* and taking a *boomerang*," and so on.

Private Eye

Number of Players	4 or more
Object	To observe the most changes that players deliberately make in their appearance
Materials	paper for each player pencil for each player 1-minute timer
Playing the Game	1. One player is chosen to be "it." One of the other players volunteers to serve as timekeeper. 2. "It" stands in front of the rest of the group for one minute. All the rest of the players observe him as carefully as they can. 3. "It" then leaves the room and quickly changes five to ten things about his appearance. For example, he might roll up his sleeves, put his watch on the opposite arm, untie a shoe, or change a ring to a different finger. "It" then returns to the room and stands in front of the group again. 4. The other players then have three minutes to write down all the changes they notice. 5. After time is up, "it" lists all the changes he made. Players score two points for each change they noticed. They lose one point for each thing they incorrectly identify as a change. "It" gets an automatic score of ten points. 6. Play continues with a new "it" through an agreed-upon number of rounds or until all players have had a chance to be "it." The player with the most points at the end of play wins.

Concentration

Number of Players	2 to 4
Object	To capture as many cards as possible by finding and claiming pairs
Materials	deck of playing cards
Playing the Game	1. Players sit around a table. One player shuffles the deck of cards and then lays them face down in a 4-by-13 card array.
	2. The player to the left of the dealer then turns over any two cards, allowing all players to see their faces. If the two cards match—for example, if they are both sevens or both queens—the player picks them both up and claims them. Each time a player claims a match, she gets another turn.
	3. If the two overturned cards do not match, the player turns them back to their original face-down position in the same location that they were found. Players should attempt to remember locations of cards to find them again for future matches.
	4. Play continues around the table until all cards have been claimed. Each player then counts the cards she has claimed. The player who claims the most cards is the winner.
Variation	Concentration may be played with hand-made cards. The cards may be used to help children master information. Concentration works well for mathematics facts (cards could be in pairs of problems—5 X 7—and answers—35). It may also be used to reinforce language skills—vocabulary words or parts of speech, for example. Sets of cards may also review science or social studies information.

Borderlines

Number of Players	3 or more
Object	To identify all the states or countries bordering a particular state or country
Materials	U.S. or world map paper for each player pencil for each player 1-minute timer
Playing the Game	1. Players choose one person to serve as game leader. The leader chooses any state in the United States and calls it out. He then starts the timer. Players may agree to use a longer time limit if one minute seems too short. 2. The other players visualize the state on the map. They try to write down within the time limit all the states that border it. 3. When time expires, the leader reads out the bordering states. Players score one point for each state they listed correctly. They lose two points for each state they have listed incorrectly. 4. The leader then passes the map to the person on his left, who serves as the leader for the next round of the game.
Variation	Instead of a U.S. map, players may use a world map. Players may decide to focus on one continent or use the entire globe as their playing field.

Adapted with permission of Sterling Publishing Co., Inc., New York, N.Y. from *Great Party Games for Grownups* by Phil Wiswell, © 1981 by Sterling Publishing Co., Inc.

Arty Dots

Number of Players	2 or more
Object	To make an interesting drawing from a group of dots another player has provided
Materials	white paper pencils, pens, crayons, markers, or other drawing materials 5-minute timer or watch
Playing the Game	1. Each player uses a pencil to make ten to twenty-five dots on a piece of paper. The dots may be placed anywhere on the paper. 2. Players then pass their papers to the left, or simply exchange papers with others at random. 3. Each player now has five minutes to use the dots on the paper she has received to draw something—an animal, a person, an object, or a scene. Players may embellish their drawings as much as they like. 4. When everyone has finished drawing, each player should share her artwork with the other players and receive their admiration.

Source: *The World Book of Children's Games,* by Arnold Arnold, New York, World Publishing, 1972. Used with permission.

Face 2 Face

Number of Players	2
Object	To guess an opponent's three-letter word
Materials	unlined paper pencil Scrabble tiles 2-minute timer

Playing the Game

1. One player serves as timekeeper. Each player draws one letter from a bag of Scrabble tiles. Each player must keep this letter secret from the other. After both players have drawn, the timekeeper starts the timer.

2. Each player thinks of a three-letter word. The word must include the letter that the player has drawn.

3. Each player then has the remainder of the two minutes to create a drawing of a face. The drawing must incorporate the three letters of the word somewhere within it. For example, the letter *e* could become a nostril, or an *m* could become part of an eyebrow.

4. After two minutes, the players exchange drawings. Each player has 3 minutes to identify the other's hidden word. There is no limit to the number of guesses a player can make. The first player to identify the other's word is the winner.

This game was created by Kate Miller, Genevieve Plentl, and Octavia Siegel-Hawley in December 1995 and is used with their permission.

Bibliography

Agostini, Franco, and Nicola Alberto DeCarlo. 1985. *Intelligence Games*. New York: Simon and Schuster.

Arnold, Arnold. 1972. *The World Book of Children's Games*. New York: World Publishing.

Brandreth, Gyles. 1981. *The World's Best Indoor Games*. New York: Pantheon.

———. 1983. *The Book of Solo Games*. New York: Harper and Row.

———. 1986. *Word Games*. New York: Harper and Row.

Conway, John. 1976. *On Numbers and Games*. Academic Press.

Espy, Willard. 1972. *The Game of Words*. New York: Grossett and Dunlap.

———. 1975. *An Almanac of Words at Play*. New York: Crown.

———. 1985. *A Children's Almanac of Words at Play*. New York: Crown.

Fleugelman, Andrew, ed. 1976. *The New Games Book*. Garden City, N.Y.: Dolphin.

Gregson, Bob. 1982. *The Incredible Indoor Games Book*. Belmond, Calif.: Pitman Learning.

Harbin, E. O. 1954. *Games of Many Nations*. New York: Abingdon Press.

Holt, Michael. 1992. *Math Puzzles and Games*. Dorset Press.

Holt, Michael, and Ronald Ridout. 1972. *The Big Book of Puzzles*. London: Longman Group.

Maguire, Jack. 1990. *Hopscotch, Hangman, Hot Potato, and Ha Ha Ha*. New York: Prentice Hall.

Murray, H. J. R. 1978. *A History of Board Games Other Than Chess*. New York: Hacker Art.

Orlick, Terry. 1978. *The Cooperative Sports and Games Book*. New York: Pantheon.

———. 1982. *The Second Cooperative Sports and Games Book*. New York: Pantheon.

Parlett, David. 1981. *Botticelli and Beyond: Over 100 of the World's Best Word Games*. New York: Pantheon.

Provenzo, Asterie Baker, and Eugene F. Provenzo Jr. 1990. *Favorite Board Games You Can Make and Play*. New York: Dover.

Rohnke, Karl. 1984. *Silver Bullets*. Dubuque, Iowa: Kendall/Hunt.

———. 1989. *Cowstails and Cobras II*. Dubuque, Iowa: Kendall/Hunt.

Schmittberger, R. Wayne. 1992. *New Rules for Classic Games*. New York: John Wiley.

Wiswell, Phil. 1981. *Great Party Games for Grownups*. New York: Sterling.

Alphabetical Index of Games